Audrey Ellis

Cooking for Your Outline Slimming in Spring Summer, Autumn, Winter

WITH DECORATIONS BY KATE WEBBER

HUTCHINSON BENHAM

Acknowledgements

Food photography: Roger Tuff
Additional recipes and food preparation: Norma Miller
Nutrition consultant: Sarah Nolan

The author and publishers also thank the following for
their help in supplying props and kitchen equipment for
the book:

The Craftsman Potter's Shop
Elizabeth David Ltd
Divertimenti
David Mellor
The Neal Street Shop
Christopher Wray's Lighting Emporium

Hutchinson Benham Limited
3 Fitzroy Square, London W1P 6JD

An imprint of the Hutchinson Group

London Melbourne Sydney Auckland
Wellington Johannesburg and agencies
throughout the world

First published 1977
© Text Van den Berghs Ltd 1977
© Decorations Hutchinson Benham Ltd 1977

Set in Linotype Bembo

Printed in Great Britain at *The
Benham Press* by William Clowes & Sons
Limited, Colchester and Beccles

ISBN 0 09 131931 5

Contents

Introduction   4
Sociable slimming – Know about nutrition –
Measure up to exercise – Create a new
eating pattern – Meal planning with
imagination – How Outline can help you
Basic Recipes   10

Spring
Starters   22
Main Meals   25
Light Meals   30
Desserts   31
Spring Ideas   35

Summer
Starters   42
Main Meals   44
Light Meals   50
Desserts   52
Summer Ideas   55

Autumn
Starters   62
Main Meals   65
Light Meals   69
Desserts   73
Autumn Ideas   75

Winter
Starters   82
Main Meals   84
Light Meals   90
Desserts   92
Winter Ideas   95

Take entertaining in your stride   96
Three Diet Plans   100
Your Guide to Joules and Calories 104
The Outline Slimming Bureau   105
Joule/Calorie Chart   106
Index of Recipes   112

Introduction

How many of us cherish a secret dream that life would become better, happier and more exciting if we could only lose a little weight? Yet, we are never quite prepared to follow a serious plan which would achieve this longed-for result. That's because the very thought of 'eating to rule' is rather depressing and seems to set you apart from family and friends who have no need to deny themselves the pleasure of devouring all the food they want.

An eating plan you approach as a penance frequently fails, whereas a plan that is fun to follow (whatever the season) is most likely to succeed. The excess weight may not drop away as quickly but the effect is more likely to last. Unsightly bulges are a constant reminder of your inability to deal with a basic problem, for which you can only blame yourself. No wonder if your expression is marred by a worried frown and little lines of discontent. The moment your clothes feel more comfortable, your outline appears more attractive in the mirror, and you begin to feel fitter, your morale receives a tremendous boost. Trimming your figure can make an amazing difference to your face – you may even smile more often. Feeling pleased with your achievement actually does make you look better.

No one likes to be out of style. Whatever the current fashion in clothes, today's look is a slim look. Overweight has long since ceased to be admired as a measure of beauty, wealth or status.

Sociable slimming

People who are the right weight are obviously more likely to be healthy than their counterparts who weigh more. That is the sensible way by which beauty and desirability are now judged. Certainly for this reason alone, modern meals are often pared down to three courses at the most, even on very formal occasions. Recipes which women love to cut out and keep are just as often for super salads as for rich desserts. There is never any need for a conscientious dieter to feel out of step because the latest trends in cooking are to help him or her reduce an excessive calorie load.

Know about nutrition

It takes courage to weigh yourself and then look at a chart which confirms that you are heavier than you should be. Unfortunately there is no magic wand you can wave to reduce your weight without eating differently and eating less, at least for a time. That flabby layer of fat you want to lose represents an excess intake of food and drink in the past. If your weight is still rising you must reduce your eating, and perhaps drinking, to keep your weight steady, and reduce it even more to lose weight. In theory, you could either eat less or take more exercise. But since energetic activities tend to stimulate your appetite, the only practical solution is to cut down your intake considerably and take extra exercise if you can.

Here are the points you need to consider carefully before starting a weight reducing diet, to ensure success:

1. Check with your doctor that all is fine for you to go ahead with a weight reducing diet. Your doctor could well have some personal advice to offer regarding the weight loss target you should set yourself.

2. Think through the advantages *you* will gain by slimming. Write your aims down so you can refer to them again if your resolve weakens after a few weeks of dieting – we all go through the doldrums at some time so prepare yourself in advance to think positively about how much you will enjoy being slim.

3. Get yourself genned up on nutrition. It will help you now and in the future to plan your eating and drinking to stay slim always. The energy (calories) in what we eat and drink is now being measured in a different way. What we know as one calorie (1 kilocalorie) under the new system becomes 4.2 joules (kilojoules). See note on page 104.

A well planned diet will contain only a few starchy or sugary foods such as jam, biscuits, pastry and steamed puddings which contain carbohydrates. Such items provide a lot of energy but do little to protect and keep your body healthy.

The richest sources of energy come from fats such as butter, margarine, oil, cream and the fat in cheese and meat. Any amount of energy eaten in excess of daily energy requirements goes into store in unlovely places on your figure. Overeating by as little as 2% (210 kilojoules or 50 kilocalories) daily over five years can result in a woman gaining 13kg (2 stone) in weight.

However, besides producing energy, the food you eat also provides essential body building and protecting elements important even when you are slimming. Proteins, needed for new body cells, are found in meat, fish, eggs and cheese and to a surprising extent in such foods as dried beans, the useful pulses which are, unfortunately, also stacked with carbo-hydrates. So from an energy point of view you are better off obtaining more of your protein from lean meat than from baked beans. One advantage of counting joules or calories is that your diet can be flexible enough to include such old favourites from time to time. What a boon it is that fruits and vegetables are relatively low in energy and provide a range of necessary vitamins and minerals. They can be included in most of our meals in delicious ways. Vitamins and minerals are vital to protect the health and functioning of the body. A varied diet can provide for all our needs. You might not remain healthy for long on a diet consisting solely of peanuts and water. It is more possible on a diet of peanuts and orange juice – but how dreary.

If you make up your menus with the help of seasonal recipes, hints and ideas in this book your diet will be far from boring, and if you follow one of the plans given on pages 103–4 it will be nutritionally sound and keep you radiantly healthy while you are gradually losing the desired amount of weight. We all vary in the amount we eat and the foods we enjoy. Flexibility is the key word; if you find you are losing more quickly than you need, give yourself the luxury of a dessert which might other-wise have been forbidden – or if the scales are not in your favour, be a little stricter with yourself.

Measure up to exercise

Your motto should be 'gently does it' when you use exercise as an aid to becoming a new trimmer you. Moving lazy muscles which have been relaxing for years can be a painful business if you try to do too much. The fact that you persevere bravely even though your muscles ache does not mean that you are achieving miracles. Simple non-strenuous exercises, performed faithfully every day even if only for a few minutes, do bring results in the end. A quick burst of frantic activity, followed by a long drink and a rest will probably achieve very little.

There are many misunderstandings about the role of exercise in losing weight. Certainly, you might have to run for miles to lose anything the scales would show. Energetic exercise also has the disadvantage of building up your appetite so that you will feel really hungry afterwards unless you consume extra food. But this is not what exercise is all about from the slimmer's point of view. First of all, choose a few movements planned to whittle your waist, roll away lumps from your hips, firm up your thighs and trim your tummy. Perform your daily dozen first thing in the morning for just five minutes, or last thing at night if it suits you better, but get right down to it. Really bend your knees and swing your body round. No one can exercise properly in restricting clothes, remember. Make sure you have space and privacy. When you really get going it would be a pity to break a favourite vase or bruise your hand on a table.

Walking is the best and easiest exercise of all because it is so much part of our daily lives that we hardly notice doing it. It makes use of just the muscles essential to a good posture – something which in itself makes you look trimmer and therefore slimmer. Muscle tone is important because it will eventually reduce your measurements. Since we judge appearance much more with the eye than with figures on a scale, everyone will congratulate you on how much weight you have lost, even if the general effect is as much due to better posture and muscle control. Try to make a positive effort to run your errands yourself, even if it means going upstairs to fetch a book or going out to post a letter. Cycling to work is better than riding in a car and if you travel by bus it helps to walk to a stop further away from home before boarding.

Create a new eating pattern

Whatever your former eating pattern it obviously has had disadvantages for you. While slimming, you have an ideal opportunity to adopt new eating habits that take into account the amount of food you need and how often and when you like to eat.

Many people today find it convenient to go without breakfast but more than make up for the lack of one by taking a biscuit or two with their coffee mid-morning, and a late supper at night. It would be much better to eat a nourishing breakfast including an egg and some fruit or alternatively take a low-fat yogurt and a piece of fruit to work with you.

Some people have a natural preference for the big meal of the day around noon and a small meal later. Others like to take their main meal at the later time, and eat sparingly in the middle of the day. For this reason the suggested meal plans are very flexible. For those who prefer to split up the amount they eat between two similar meals, the starter or dessert can be paired up with the light meal of the day.

Be honest with yourself about your weak spots. Boredom is frequently a dieter's worst enemy. Do not succumb to the temptation of snatching a surreptitious sweet or chocolate. Provide yourself with a nibble bowl containing your favourite crisp raw salad vegetables such as carrot, radish, green pepper or pickled vegetables – gherkins and onions. Then you can always satisfy a genuine pang of hunger.

In warm weather make flavoured ice cubes with sugar free fruit squashes – they are deliciously refreshing.

Cheating is something few dieters can avoid. If you cannot take some foods in a small measured amount without an overwhelming desire for more, it is better to cut them out completely. The occasional extra indulgence can be corrected by deliberately eating less the day afterwards, or better still anticipating it by eating less the day before. But don't let it go beyond that and allow the insidious habit of overeating to creep up on you again. Fortunately, one does quite quickly become accustomed to eating less, and it no longer requires such a conscious effort.

Once you have lost enough weight, your aim should be to

stay steady. Do not in a moment of triumph decide to go back to your old eating habits, but gradually increase the amount you eat, taking care to weigh yourself every week and make sure that the scale is not sneaking up again.

Meal planning with imagination

The image of a dieter's meals is all too often conjured up as a lettuce leaf and tiny cube of cheese, side by side on a vast and otherwise empty plate. This is a totally wrong conception. The food should always be attractively presented on just the right-sized plate or in a dish to accommodate it comfortably. However, you would do well to banish your largest dinner plates to the back of the cupboard permanently.

Meal planning means exactly what it says; working out a pleasing combination of different foods in terms of flavour, texture and colour. Variety is the spice of life in eating most meals, although many people happily consume the same standard breakfast every day. Salads, for example, can become dispiriting if they consist always of limp lettuce. Even crisp lettuce can become boring if it invariably has the same partner of sliced cucumber or quartered tomatoes. Introduce many others: a crisp raw vegetable that is usually eaten cooked, like cauliflower florets; or a fresh fruit which contrasts well with a tangy salad dressing. Providing they are very thinly sliced, dark green cabbage, red cabbage, Brussels sprouts and leeks are delicious surprise ingredients for any salad, and especially useful in winter.

The way food looks tempts the taste buds before you begin eating. Fortunately most garnishes such as a single coiled anchovy fillet or halved olive add minimally to the energy content and enormously to the appeal of the dish. A sugar free carbonated drink poured over crushed ice in a pretty glass and topped with a sprig of mint is highly enjoyable.

How Outline can help you

Excessive amounts of fat contribute to weight problems. Many of us eat a fat-rich diet without realising it. For instance people who do not eat much butter frequently enjoy fried food cooked in lard or dripping. Oil is no better.

9

Outline is different. It is a low-fat spread (not a margarine) made for slimmers. It has been specially formulated to contain vitamins A and D in the same proportion as margarine, but it does not contain any milk solids. This makes it suitable for people with allergies to milk, and vegans who cannot eat any dairy produce. All the oils in Outline are derived from vegetable sources, and it is cholesterol free. Its particular interest to slimmers is that it contains only half the joules (calories) of butter or margarine. Some care must be used in cooking with it as it is an emulsion of water in a blend of natural vegetable oils. Although one cannot deep fry with Outline it is perfectly suitable for sauteing meat or vegetables for stews and casseroles, and for All-in-One soups and sauces. Use it to make a Victoria sandwich cake, choux pastry and scones for a pizza base or to make a cobbler topping. Use it instead of butter for spreading, glazing meat or fish for grilling or as a topping for cooked vegetables. It saves half the energy each time.

Basic Recipes

The quantities given for the recipe ingredients appear as metric then imperial units. A calorie count is provided for each recipe. The first figure given at the end of each recipe refers to the recipe made up with metric quantities. The second calorie value given is for the imperial version. The two values may differ slightly because we have chosen the most convenient metric equivalents, rather than exact conversions which make measuring too fiddly. For packaged goods we have given the manufacturer's exact conversion as stated on the pack (eg 113 grammes for 4 ounces instead of the easy 100 grammes).

Here is an invaluable collection of recipes you will want to use over and over again, because they form the basis of a wide range of dishes. All have been devised for easy preparation.

All-in-One Sauces

Method for All-in-One Sauces

1 Place all ingredients in a saucepan.
2 Bring to the boil over a moderate heat, stirring continuously.
3 Cook for 2–3 minutes until thickened and smooth.

POURING SAUCE

15 g (½ oz) Outline
15 g (½ oz) plain flour
275 ml (½ pint) skimmed milk
Salt and pepper

Calories 200 (205)

COATING

25 g (1 oz) Outline
25 g (1 oz) plain flour
275 ml (½ pint) skimmed milk
Salt and pepper

Calories 270 (305)

PANADA

50 g (2 oz) Outline
50 g (2 oz) plain flour

Calories 450 (510)

275 ml (½ pint) skimmed milk
Salt and pepper

Variations

Follow the basic recipes for the consistency you want but add the appropriate ingredients after the sauce has boiled.

ONION SAUCE

*2 onions, skinned, chopped and
  boiled*

Calories: pouring 255 (260)
           coating 325 (360)

PARSLEY OR MINT SAUCE

*15 ml (1 tablespoon) parsley or
  mint, chopped*

Calories: pouring 200 (205)
           coating 270 (305)

CHEESE SAUCE

75 g (3 oz) Edam cheese, grated
*2.5 ml (½ teaspoon) made
  mustard*

Calories: pouring 435 (470)
           coating 510 (570)

All-in-One Scones

225 g (8 oz) self-raising flour
5 ml (1 teaspoon) baking powder
50 g (2 oz) Outline
15 g (½ oz) castor sugar
90 ml (6 tablespoons) skimmed
  milk

} sieved together

1   Place all ingredients in a mixing bowl and mix with a fork to form a firm dough.
2   Chill for ½ hour.
3   Turn onto a lightly floured surface and knead lightly until smooth.
4   Roll and cut out 10 x 6.5 cm (2½ inch) discs using fluted or plain floured cutter.
5   Bake on the second from top shelf of a pre-heated oven (218°C 420°F Gas 7) for 12–15 minutes until risen and golden brown.

MAKES 10

Calories per scone 105 (110)

Variations

CHEESE

Omit sugar and add to the basic recipe:

100 g (4 oz) finely grated Edam
  cheese

Salt and pepper
5 ml (1 teaspoon) dry mustard

MAKES 10

Calories per scone 130 (140)

HERB

Omit sugar and add to the basic recipe:

2.5 ml (½ teaspoon) mixed
  herbs

MAKES 10

Calories per scone 130 (140)
NB. Remember to add 25 calories for every 6 g (¼ oz) Outline spread on the scones.

All-in-One Victoria Sandwich

175 g (6 oz) Outline
175 g (6 oz) castor sugar
3 large eggs
175 g (6 oz) self-raising flour ⎫ *sieved*
7.5 ml (1½ teaspoons) baking ⎬ *together*
  powder ⎭

1 Place all ingredients in a mixing bowl.
2 Beat with a wooden spoon until well mixed (2–3 minutes).
3 Divide the mixture evenly between 2 x 17.5 cm (7 inch) sandwich tins.
4 Bake in centre of pre-heated oven (160°C 325°F, Gas 3) for 35–45 minutes. Remove from tin and cool on a wire tray. Sandwich cake together and fill with your favourite slimmers' filling.

Calories for whole cake 2220 (2165)
Calories for ⅛th of cake 275 (270)
Filling suggestion: Slimmers' Jam

Variations

CHOCOLATE
Omit 25 g (1 oz) self-raising flour and replace with 25 g (1 oz) cocoa powder.

Calories for ⅛th cake 290 (280)

ORANGE OR LEMON
Add grated rind of one orange or lemon.

Calories for ⅛th of cake 275 (270)

COFFEE
Add 10 ml (2 teaspoons) instant coffee dissolved in 15 ml (1 tablespoon) boiling water and cooled.

Calories for ⅛th of cake 275 (270)

Creamy Filling

40 g (1½ oz) Outline   *75 g (3 oz) icing sugar*

Place all ingredients in a mixing bowl and beat together with a wooden spoon until well mixed.

Calories 460 (485)

GLACE ICING FOR TOP

50 g (2 oz) icing sugar
2 x 5 ml (2 teaspoons) warm
  water or orange or lemon juice

Place all ingredients together in a mixing bowl and beat with a wooden spoon until smooth.

Calories 200 (225)

Choux Pastry

150 ml (¼ pint) water
50 g (2 oz) Outline
65 g (2½ oz) plain flour } *sieved*
Pinch of salt } *together*
2 large eggs, lightly beaten

1   Place water and Outline in a small saucepan and bring to the boil over a moderate heat.
2   Remove from the heat and immediately add the sieved flour. Beat with a wooden spoon until mixture leaves the sides of the pan. Cool slightly.
3   Beat the eggs in small additions into the cooled mixture.
4   The pastry is now ready to use.

   Makes 150 ml (¼ pint) pastry
   Calories 590 (640)

Start the day well all round the year

Breakfast is the meal that has to provide energy for your activities up until noon. If you miss out on breakfast the level of glucose in your blood remains low. The result? Irritability, a feeling of tiredness, lack of mental alertness and possibly avoidable muddles in your work. Worst of all a craving for a high carbohydrate food which would release instant energy: chocolate, biscuits, buns, sweets to chew. All good breakfasts include some protein such as a boiled or poached egg, a supply of vitamin C and a small amount of carbohydrate to get the general metabolism (and this includes the digestive system) to work.

Nagging hunger pangs and listlessness are signs that you need a meal like this long before the lunch break. If lack of time to prepare breakfast in the morning is your genuine excuse, remember you do not need to cook breakfast – fruit juice and cereal or yogurt will be fine.

Spring

Often, spring is the best time to slim because it is a season of reawakening and renewed energy. All round you nature is stirring after the long winter sleep. Buds breaking, birds singing again and your thoughts turning to those revealing summer clothes at the back of the wardrobe. This is the time to put them in order and alter the length of hems if necessary. Let the brighter mornings tempt you out of bed earlier to begin a new programme of whittle-away exercises to back up the diet, and give yourself a weight-loss goal. It helps to have a date in mind, whether an early holiday, a family reunion at Easter, or a wedding. Here is a thoughtfully chosen selection of recipes to help you enjoy every meal while you are losing weight. Brown eggs, baby carrots, delicate fresh fish and tender pink rhubarb – just part of the encouragement spring brings to diet menus at this green and gorgeous time of the year.

Consommé with Tropical Garnish, Chicken Liver Pâté, Fish Mousse and Avocado and Grapefruit Cups

Gammon with Fresh Apricot Sauce, Breton Lamb, Hot Baked Chicken with Artichoke Salad and Florentine Fish with Parsley Pats

Spring Specials

BREAKFAST IDEAS

All these can be taken with tea or coffee and skimmed milk.

1. Egg-in-the-nest: Remove the crusts and cut a disc from the centre of a slice of slimmers' bread, using a small glass or biscuit cutter. Dip the bread quickly into cold water (do not let it get soggy) and fry gently on one side in 15 g (½ oz) melted Outline until golden. Turn over and break an egg into the centre. Season with salt and pepper to taste and fry until the egg is set.
2. One small apple and 25 g (1 oz) breakfast cereal served with 150 ml (¼ pint) skimmed milk and artificial sweetener to taste.
3. Half a grapefruit and 2 slices of slimmers' bread, toasted and thinly spread with Outline, topped with 50 g (2 oz) grilled cod's roe.
4. Zesty orange juice: Beat up 1 egg in 100 ml (4 fl oz) unsweetened orange juice. Serve with 1 slice toast thinly spread with Outline and yeast extract.
5. Half a grapefruit, segmented, and the flesh mixed with 75 g (3 oz) cottage cheese, seasoning, and 1 well-grilled rasher of back bacon, diced. Pile back into the grapefruit shell and serve with 1 thin crispbread.

NIBBLES

All these can be taken in addition to your daily calorie allowance, but don't make a meal of them.

1. A nibble bowl of crisp vegetable bites to prepare and keep in an airtight container in the refrigerator: chicory leaves, celery sticks, shredded white cabbage, bean sprouts.
2. Chinese cabbage: Shredded white cabbage tossed with seasoned tomato juice and soy sauce.
3. Cheese charms: 15 ml (1 tablespoon) cottage cheese sprinkled with caraway seeds, paprika pepper and salt.
4. One crispbread thinly spread with yeast extract.
5. Fruit jelly made with sugar-free fruit drink and gelatine.

Top left, Fruit Jelly with Creamy Topping   *Centre right*, Coffee Chiffon
Top right, Banana Ring   *Bottom left*, Mandarin Eclair
Centre left, Rhubarb and Ginger Crunch   *Bottom right*, Choux Delight

Starters

Consomme with Tropical Garnish

(See photograph page 17)

2 beef stock cubes
900 ml (1 ½ pints) boiling water
75 g (3 oz) stewing steak, cubed
1 small onion, 1 small carrot
5 ml (1 teaspoon) tomato purée
5 ml (1 teaspoon) lime ★ juice
30 ml (2 tablespoons) sherry

TROPICAL GARNISH

15 ml (1 tablespoon) grated fresh
  coconut
Few thin strips lime rind
1 small piece preserved ginger,
  finely sliced

1   Dissolve the stock cubes in the boiling water in a saucepan.
    Add the meat, onion, carrot, tomato purée and lime juice
    and stir well. Bring back to the boil, cover and simmer for
    1 hour. Cool.
2   Strain, chill and skim off fatty layer.
3   Reheat with the sherry, add the ingredients for the garnish
    and simmer for 5 minutes.
4   Serve in soup cups, dividing the garnish between them
    with the aid of a slotted draining spoon.

SERVES 4   Calories per portion 80 (85)

*If limes are unavailable this is just as delicious using lemons instead.

Avocado and Grapefruit Cups

(See photograph page 17)

2 grapefruit
2 avocado pears
Lemon juice

Salt and pepper
60 ml (4 tablespoons) port
4 sprigs of watercress

1   Halve the grapefruit with a zigzag action and remove the
    segments. Retain grapefruit shells.
2   Peel the avocados and remove the stones. Roughly chop
    the flesh and sprinkle with lemon juice, salt and pepper.

22

3   Place the grapefruit segments and avocado flesh back into the grapefruit shells.
4   Pour 15 ml (1 tablespoon) port over each and decorate with watercress.

SERVES 4

Calories per portion 160 (160)

Fish Mousse

(See photograph page 17)

175 g (6 oz) fresh or canned
  salmon
15 cm (6 inch) length cucumber,
  peeled
150 ml (¼ pint) All-in-One
  coating sauce (see basic recipe
  page 11)

15 g (½ oz) gelatine
60 ml (4 tablespoons) slimmers'
  salad dressing
Salt and pepper
Egg white
4 lemon twists to garnish

1   Poach the salmon in water to cover for 12–15 minutes. Remove skin and flake. Reserve the fish stock. If using canned salmon, remove contents, keeping the juice.
2   Halve cucumber lengthwise and scoop out the seeds. Dice the flesh and cook for 5 minutes in the reserved liquid. Remove the cooked cucumber with a slotted draining spoon and liquidize with the salmon and 30 ml (2 tablespoons) of the stock.
3   Dissolve the gelatine in 30 ml (2 tablespoons) more hot stock or reserved juice.
4   Make sauce. Stir in fish mixture, salad dressing and dissolved gelatine. Season to taste.
5   Whisk the egg white until stiff and fold into the fish mixture.
6   Divide between 4 individual soufflé or glass dishes (or wineglasses) and chill until set.
7   Serve garnished with lemon twists.

SERVES 8   Calories per portion 160 (160)

Chicken Liver Paté

(See photograph page 17)

1 small onion, finely chopped
25 g (1 oz) Outline
225 g (8 oz) chicken livers
20 g (¾ oz) flour
175 g (6 oz) curd cheese (if

unavailable use cottage cheese)
15 ml (1 tablespoon) sherry
1 clove garlic, crushed
Salt and pepper

1   Fry onion gently in Outline to soften (4–5 minutes) and then remove from the pan.
2   Trim livers, wash, dry and toss in the flour to coat. Put in the pan, cover and cook gently for 6–8 minutes.
3   When cooked, chop with the onions and pass through a sieve. Add cheese, sherry, garlic and seasoning and blend well together. Chill in refrigerator.
4   Serve with triangles of toast spread with a little Outline.

SERVES 4 Calories per portion without toast 185 (185)

Baked Celery in Sherry Sauce

4 small heads or large 'hearts' of celery
50 g (2 oz) Outline
4 spring onions, trimmed
5 ml (1 teaspoon) yeast extract

30 ml (2 tablespoons) boiling water
60 ml (4 tablespoons) sherry
Salt and pepper
15 ml (1 tablespoon) toasted breadcrumbs

1   Trim the celery portions and slice through lengthwise from the top almost to the base. Spread half the Outline in the bottom of a small shallow ovenproof dish and lay the celery portions closely side by side on this.
2   Finely chop the onions and sprinkle over the top.
3   Dissolve the yeast extract in the boiling water, add the sherry, season to taste, stir and pour over the celery.
4   Cover lightly with foil, and cook in the oven at 190°C 375°F, Gas 5, for 30 minutes.
5   Remove the foil, and sprinkle with the crumbs. Melt the remaining Outline and drizzle over the top. Return uncovered to the oven for a further 20 minutes.
6   Serve hot or cold.

SERVES 4 Calories per portion 80 (85)

Main Meals

Gammon with Fresh Apricot Sauce

(See photograph pages 18-19)

4 x 100 g (4 oz) gammon steaks
25 g (1 oz) Outline

SAUCE

225 g (8 oz) apricots
150 ml (¼ pint) water
15 ml (1 tablespoon) vinegar

2.5 ml (½ teaspoon) ground
    allspice
Salt and pepper
1 chicken stock cube
30 ml (2 tablespoons) slimmers'
    apricot jam
Watercress to garnish

1   Snip the rind on the gammon steaks and spread one side
    with half the Outline. Grill under moderate heat for 7–10
    minutes.
2   Turn them over, spread with the remaining Outline and
    grill until the fat is golden brown and lean meat cooked
    through.
3   Meanwhile make the sauce. Halve and stone the apricots.
    Place them in a saucepan with the water, vinegar, spice,
    crumbled stock cube and seasoning to taste. Poach gently
    until the apricots are tender. Stir in the apricot jam, until
    completely melted.
4   Place the gammon steaks on a warm serving dish. Spoon a
    little sauce over each steak and hand the remainder sepa-
    rately. Surround with a border of watercress sprigs.
5   With each portion serve 100 g (4 oz) chopped spinach,
    with 6 g (¼ oz) Outline, melted and poured over all 4
    portions.

SERVES 4

Calories per portion with vegetables 320 (355)

Slim Beef Casserole

1 head of celery
1 large cooking apple, peeled
450 g (1 lb) lean braising steak, cubed
15 ml (1 tablespoon) seasoned flour
40 g (1½ oz) Outline
1 large onion, peeled and chopped

225 g (8 oz) firm white cabbage, shredded
1 beef stock cube
425 ml (¾ pint) boiling water
Good pinch ground cloves
Salt and pepper
2 bay leaves

1　Trim the celery and cut into short lengths. Core and slice the apple.
2　Lightly dust the meat with the seasoned flour and brown gently all over in the Outline.
3　Add the prepared vegetables and sauté in Outline for 5 minutes, stirring frequently.
4　Dissolve the stock cube in the boiling water, add the spice and seasoning.
5　Place half the meat and vegetable mixture in an ovenproof casserole, cover with apple slices, then top with the remaining meat and vegetable mixture. Pour over the seasoned stock and add the bay leaves.
6　Cover and cook at 180°C 350°F, Gas 4, for about 2 hours, until the beef is tender. Remove the bay leaves and adjust the seasoning if necessary.
7　Serve each person with a portion of the casserole and a 100 g (4 oz) baked potato, slashed and topped with 15 g (½ oz) Outline.

SERVES 4　Calories per portion with potato 460 (480)

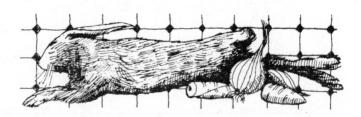

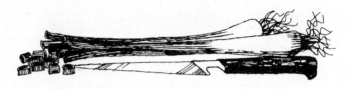

Hot Baked Chicken with Artichoke Salad

(See photograph pages 18–19)

2 oranges
50 g (2 oz) Outline
4 chicken portions, without skin
Salt and pepper

SALAD

225 g (8 oz) can artichoke hearts, drained

1 hard-boiled egg
60 ml (4 tablespoons) slimmer's salad dressing
100 g (4 oz) cottage cheese, sieved
1 small lettuce, shredded

1   Finely grate the rind from the oranges and squeeze the juice from one. Mix the rind with the Outline. Season.
2   Place the chicken portions, flesh side down, in a small roasting tin and bake in a moderately hot oven 190°C 375°F, Gas 5, for 20 minutes. Turn the portions over and spread with the orange–Outline mixture. Return to the oven for a further 20 minutes, or until cooked through.
3   Meanwhile, make the salad. Halve or quarter the artichoke hearts, as preferred. Roughly chop the egg. Peel and segment the remaining orange. Beat the salad dressing and sieved cottage cheese together and gradually beat in the reserved orange juice. Season to taste. Fold in the chopped egg and artichoke.
4   Place the lettuce on a shallow serving dish. Mound up the salad in the centre and surround it with the 4 hot chicken portions. Arrange with orange segments between the portions and serve at once.
5   Serve each portion with 100 g (4 oz) runner beans.

SERVES 4   Calories per portion with vegetables 400 (410)

Breton Lamb

(See photograph pages 18–19)

150 g (5 oz) haricot beans
(soaked overnight)
1 large onion, peeled
Salt and pepper
Bouquet garni
1–1½ kg (2–3 lb) leg lamb

1 clove garlic, peeled and cut into
slivers
15 g (½ oz) Outline
1 small onion, chopped
2 large tomatoes, peeled and
chopped

1   Put soaked beans and whole onion in a large saucepan with seasoning and bouquet garni. Cover with water and bring slowly to the boil. Simmer for about one hour until beans are soft.
2   Diagonally cut surface of meat and press in slivers of garlic. Dust surface with salt and pepper and rub over half the Outline. Place on rack in roasting tin and roast in pre-heated oven 190°C 375°F, Gas 5, allowing 20 minutes per ½ kg (1 lb) and 20 minutes over.
3   Strain beans and onion and keep warm; when meat is cooked remove to a dish and keep warm. Remove 15 ml (1 tablespoon) of meat juices from roasting tin.
4   In a separate pan melt the remainder of Outline. Add small chopped onion, tomatoes and boiled onion. Simmer gently until softened and season to taste. Add reserved meat juice and cooked beans and pour over meat.

SERVES 4   Calories per portion 450 (445)

Stuffed Mackerel

4 x 200 g (7 oz) mackerel

STUFFING

100 g (4 oz) cottage cheese
Salt and pepper

5 ml (1 teaspoon) mixed herbs
Rind and juice 1 lemon
100 g (4 oz) soft breadcrumbs
1 standard egg

1   Clean mackerel and remove the backbones.
2   Mix all stuffing ingredients together and stuff the fish.

3   Wrap each mackerel in a foil parcel. Bake in centre of a pre-heated oven 190°C 375°F, Gas 5, for 30 minutes.
4   Serve each mackerel with a 175 g (6 oz) baked jacket potato, topped with 15 g (½ oz) Outline, and a baked tomato.

SERVES 4   Calories per portion with vegetables 600 (645)

Cheesey Pasta with Kidneys

225 g (8 oz) vermicelli or other type of pasta
6 g (¼ oz) Outline
75 g (3 oz) Edam cheese, coarsely grated
275 g (10 oz) lamb's kidneys, skinned, halved and cored
15 g (½ oz) Outline

2 medium onions, peeled and sliced
25 g (1 oz) streaky bacon, diced
175 g (6 oz) carrots, sliced
15 g (½ oz) cornflour
425 ml (¾ pint) beef stock
2.5 ml (½ teaspoon) mixed herbs

1   Cook the pasta in boiling salted water for 6–8 minutes. Drain and toss in the Outline and cheese. Form in a ring in an ovenproof dish. Bake near the top of a pre-heated oven 200°C 400°F, Gas 6, for 30 minutes.
2   Place remaining ingredients in a saucepan, stirring continuously, bring to the boil and simmer for 25–30 minutes.
3   Pour the kidney mixture inside the pasta ring.

SERVES 4   Calories per portion 420 (435)

Light Meals

Ocean Toasties

8 slices slimmers' bread, toasted
25 g (1 oz) Outline
227 g (8 oz) can pilchards in
  tomato sauce

2 standard eggs
6 g (¼ oz) Outline
30 ml (2 tablespoons) skimmed
  milk

1   Spread the toast with Outline and top with the pilchards.
    Place under the grill for a few minutes.
2   Make scrambled egg with the eggs, Outline and skimmed
    milk.
3   Top the pilchards with the egg mixture and serve
    immediately.

    2 toasties per person

SERVES 4   Calories per serving 235 (240)

Florentine Fish with Parsley Pats

(See photograph pages 18–19)

1 small bunch parsley
100 g (4 oz) Outline
30 ml (2 tablespoons) lemon
  juice
150 ml (¼ pint) water
1 small onion, sliced

Salt and pepper
4 x 100 g (4 oz) steaks of halibut
  or haddock
1 egg white
225 g (8 oz) cooked chopped
  spinach

1   Separate the parsley sprigs from the stalks and chop the
    sprigs. Reserve parsley stalks.
2   Beat the Outline together with 5 ml (1 teaspoon) of the
    lemon juice and the chopped parsley. Form into a roll,
    wrap in greaseproof paper or foil and chill while you cook
    the fish.

3   Heat together in a saucepan the water, remaining lemon
     juice, onion, parsley stalks and seasoning.
4   Place the fish steaks in a small ovenproof dish, pour over
     the hot stock and cook in a moderately hot oven 190°C,
     375°F, Gas 5, for about 20 minutes, until the flesh parts
     easily from the bone.
5   Whisk the egg white until stiff and fold into the hot
     spinach. Spread a bed of spinach on a warm serving dish.
     Arrange the fish steaks on this and top with thinly sliced
     parsley pats cut from the chilled roll.
6   Serve each portion with one heaped 15 ml spoon (1 table-
     spoon) whipped potato, made with skimmed milk.

SERVES 4   Calories per portion with potato 280 (300)

Desserts

Rhubarb and Ginger Crunch

(See photograph page 20)

450 g (1 lb) rhubarb, washed and   2.5 ml (½ teaspoon) ground
   sliced   ginger
Artificial liquid sweetener   25 g (1 oz) Outline
4 slices slimmers' bread, crumbed

1   Cook rhubarb with a little water until tender.
2   Add sweetener to taste.
3   Place in an ovenproof dish and keep warm.
4   Mix together crumbs and ginger.
5   Melt Outline in a frying pan and toss crumbs in it until
     golden.
6   Scatter crumbs on top of rhubarb and serve immediately.

SERVES 4   Calories per portion 75 (75)

Coffee Chiffon

(See photograph page 20)

2 eggs, separated
150 ml (¼ pint) hot strong black
  coffee
10 ml (2 teaspoons) gelatine
30 ml (2 teaspoons) skimmed
  milk powder

Artificial liquid sweetener to
  taste
15 g (½ oz) chocolate curls
Rum essence to taste

1 Place the egg yolks in a basin and beat until smooth and
  creamy.
2 Reserve a little hot coffee and use to dissolve the gelatine.
3 Dissolve the skimmed milk powder in the remaining coffee and gradually beat into the egg yolks. Add sweetener
  to taste.
4 Place the basin over hot water and stir until the mixture
  thickens sufficiently to coat the back of the spoon. Stir in
  the dissolved gelatine with rum essence to taste. Cool.
5 Stiffly whisk the egg whites and fold into the custard
  mixture when it is cool and on the point of setting.
6 Spoon into 4 sundae glasses and top with chocolate curls.

SERVES 4   Calories per portion 90 (90)

Fruit Jellies with Creamy Topping

(See photograph page 20)

311 g (11 oz) can mandarin
  oranges
1 orange-flavoured packet jelly
150 ml (¼ pint) boiling water

CREAMY TOPPING

2.5 ml (½ teaspoon) gelatine

15 ml (1 tablespoon) hot water
15 ml (1 tablespoon) skimmed
  milk powder
50 ml (2 fl oz) cold water
5 ml (1 teaspoon) castor sugar
Few drops lemon juice
Few drops vanilla essence

1 Drain the mandarins, dissolve jelly in boiling water and
  add the mandarin juice. Leave to set until syrupy. Stir in
  the mandarins. Pour into 4 sundae glasses and leave to set.

2   Make the Creamy Topping. In a small basin dissolve the
    gelatine in the hot water and stir in remaining ingredients.
    Beat until soft peaks form. Pipe rosettes or drop spoonfuls
    of the topping on the set jellies.
3   Serve each person with one sundae glass.

SERVES 4   Calories per portion with topping 160 (160)
           Creamy Topping recipe alone 80 (80)

Choux Delights

(See photograph page 20)

½ quantity choux pastry (see
  basic recipe page 14)
180 ml (12 tablespoons) vanilla
  ice-cream

225 g (8 oz) strawberries, sliced
90 ml (6 tablespoons) raspberry
  sauce, warmed

1   Make choux pastry.
2   Place 90 ml (6 tablespoons) of the mixture on a wet baking
    sheet.
3   Bake near the top of a pre-heated oven 220°C 375°F, Gas 5,
    for 15–20 minutes.
4   Slit base of buns and cool.
5   When cold fill the buns with ice-cream and sliced straw-
    berries.
6   Pour 15 ml (1 tablespoon) raspberry sauce over each bun
    before serving.

SERVES 6   Calories per bun 190 (195)

Banana Rings

(See photograph page 20)

½ quantity choux pastry (see
  basic recipe page 14)
1 ripe banana
60 ml (4 tablspoons) warm
  custard made with skimmed

milk and artificial liquid
  sweetener to taste
Slimmers' apricot jam

33

1 Pipe the choux pastry into 6 rings. Bake, split and cool (See step 3, Choux Delights, page 33).
2 Mash the banana and beat in the sweetened custard. Cool.
3 Fill the rings with the banana mixture, and glaze the tops with apricot jam.

SERVES 6   Calories per ring 70 (75)

Mandarin Eclairs

(See photograph page 20)

½ quantity choux pastry
  (See basic recipe page 14)
311 g (11 oz) can mandarin
  orange segments in natural
  juice

5 ml (1 teaspoon) arrowroot
Liquid artificial sweetener, to
  taste
Icing sugar

1 Pipe the choux pastry into 6 fingers. Bake, split and cool (See step 3, Choux Delights, page 33).
2 Drain mandarins reserving 90 ml (6 tablespoons) juice. Mix this with arrowroot and cook, stirring, in a small pan just until thick and clear. Add sweetener to taste. Stir in the drained mandarins and cool.
3 Fill the choux fingers with the mandarin mixture, and sift the tops lightly with icing sugar.

SERVES 6   Calories per éclair 80 (85)

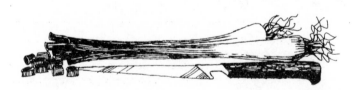

Spring Ideas

1 Keeping your hands busy diverts your mind from thoughts of reaching towards the biscuit tin. This is the time of year when so much needs to be done in the garden (if you have one), and gardening provides excellent exercise in the form of knee-bending and stretching. With the help of pots, troughs and growing bags, most people can cultivate a small patch. If not, be enterprising and offer to help a friend who has a garden.

2 Eggs are abundant and you may get tired of eating them boiled. You can actually dry-fry an egg in a non-stick pan if you break it into an egg ring greased with Outline; otherwise the white may spread out too much.

3 If stewed rhubarb becomes boring, try cooking it in various slimmers' drinks instead of water. Ginger ale or orange are particularly delicious

4 When it comes to energy content, white fish is a better investment than poultry or meat. If it is expensive, be enterprising and try the most recent arrivals on the fishmonger's slab – blue whiting, huss and coley (called saithe in some parts of the country).

Spring Drinks

ALMOND BLUSH

Fill a wineglass with slimmers' ginger ale, add a few drops of almond essence and 15 ml (1 tablespoon) unsweetened orange juice. Stir well.

ICED VANILLA COFFEE

Add a few drops of vanilla essence to a glass of chilled coffee made with skimmed milk. Add liquid sweetener to taste.

Summer

As summer approaches, our thoughts turn to luscious strawberries and peaches, delicate asparagus, and all the other mouth-watering delights of the season. In some ways, summer is the easiest time to slim because all its delectable fresh fruits and vegetables are perfectly in tune with a slimming diet. Leafy, lovely, tempting salads are not only a natural choice but absolutely at their best, and probably lowest in price, at this time of the year. Everyone is eating salads so who will guess you are choosing them to trim away unwanted weight as well as just for pleasure? Streamline your clothes to fit your new figure. Most dresses can be taken in at the side seams or by darts. It's swimsuit weather, and you may even want to brave a bikini; encouragement enough to follow your diet plan faithfully. These super recipes are here to help you enjoy all the bounty of summer while you slim.

Top left, Tomato and Tuna Jelly

Top right, Chunky Veal Soup

Bottom left, Pasta Salad with Fish

Bottom right, Herbed Cucumber Omelette

Foreground, Barbecued Pork
Pockets, Turkey Escalopes with Mint

Background, Seafood Cocktail and
Cold Courgette Salad

Summer Specials

BREAKFAST IDEAS (None over 200 Calories)

1 Make a compôte by stewing 100 g (4 oz) sliced rhubarb and
   50 g (2 oz) sliced strawberries in 100 ml (4 fl oz) unsweetened
   orange juice. Add artificial sweetener to taste. Serve with
   1 small slice of brown bread thinly spread with Outline.
2 Mix together 30 ml (2 tablespoons) rolled oats, 1 small
   orange, segmented, 1 small apple, cored and sliced, 5 ml
   (1 teaspoon) chopped walnuts and artificial sweetener to
   taste. Serve with 30 ml (2 tablespoons) natural yogurt.
3 Two small eggs, scrambled with a little skimmed milk and
   Outline.
4 One small carton low-fat natural yogurt and 1 small banana
   and 15 g (½ oz) Edam cheese.
5 One small slice of brown bread thinly spread with Outline
   and 50 g (2 oz) lean ham.

NIBBLES

All these can be taken in addition to your daily diet allowance,
but don't make a meal of them.

1 A nibble bowl of crisp vegetable bites to prepare and keep in
   an airtight container in the refrigerator: unpeeled cucumber
   slices, radishes, spring onions, lettuce heart quarters, shredded Savoy cabbage.
2 One small cooked artichoke heart.
3 Pickled cabbage with apple. Fold 15 ml (1 tablespoon)
   grated apple and 5 ml (1 teaspoon) grated onion into 30 ml
   (2 tablespoons) pickled red cabbage.
4 Ice lollies made with slimmers' fruit drink.
5 30 ml (2 tablespoons) cooked rhubarb stewed in slimmers'
   ginger ale.

Top, Black Cherry Gateau, Chocolate Fairy Cakes
and Raspberry Cheesecake
Bottom, Red and Black Currant Ice, Gooseberry
Mint Snow, Peach and Strawberry Fluff

Starters

Cold Courgette Salad

(See photograph pages 38–39)

450 g (1 lb) courgettes
40 g (1½ oz) Outline
1 clove garlic
1 medium onion, finely sliced

Salt and pepper
2 large tomatoes
15 ml (1 tablespoon) vinegar
15 ml (1 tablespoon) oil

1   Top and tail the courgettes. Dice finely. Place in a sauce-pan and pour over just sufficient boiling water to cover. Bring to the boil and simmer for 5 minutes. Drain.
2   Meanwhile, melt the Outline in a frying pan, add the garlic and onion and cook gently, stirring until transparent.
3   Add the courgettes, season to taste and cook, stirring for 5 minutes. Cool.
4   Peel the tomatoes, de-seed and roughly chop the flesh.
5   Whisk the vinegar and oil together and stir into the courgettes with the chopped tomato.
6   Divide between 4 small salad bowls.

SERVES 4   Calories per portion 90 (90)

Chilled Green Pea Soup

1 small onion
6 large lettuce leaves
450 g (1 lb) fresh or frozen peas
25 g (1 oz) Outline
30 ml (2 tablespoons) chopped
   mint

1 litre (1¾ pints) chicken stock
5 ml (1 teaspoon) sugar
Salt and pepper
30 ml (2 tablespoons) low-fat
   natural yogurt

1   Grate the onion, shred the lettuce finely and shell peas (if fresh).

2   Melt the Outline in a large saucepan, add the peas, onion,
    lettuce and half the mint. Cover and cook gently for 10
    minutes.
3   Add the stock, sugar and seasoning to taste. Cover and
    simmer for about 30–40 minutes.
4   Liquidize, pour into a bowl, stir in the yogurt and chill.
5   Serve each person with a portion of chilled soup, sprinkled
    with chopped mint.

SERVES 4   Calories per portion 125 (125)

Seafood Cocktail

(See photograph pages 38–39)

Lettuce leaves
Cucumber, sliced
4 tomatoes, sliced
225 g (8 oz) cockles
225 g (8 oz) mussels

DRESSING

150 g (5.3 oz) low-fat natural
  yogurt

10 ml (2 teaspoons) wine vinegar
30 ml (2 tablespoons) fresh mint
  or parsley, chopped
Salt and pepper
1 clove of garlic, crushed

Watercress to garnish

1   Shred the lettuce and divide between four plates.
2   Edge the lettuce with slices of cucumber and tomato.
3   Mix together the dressing ingredients.
4   Toss the cockles and mussels in a little of the dressing and
    pile onto the lettuce. Garnish with watercress and serve the
    remainder of the dressing separately.

SERVES 4   Calories per portion 110 (110)

Main Meals

Sicilian Veal Roast

1 large lemon
25 g (1 oz) Outline
Salt and pepper
½ packet parsley and thyme
  stuffing
1 egg yolk

5 ml (1 teaspoon) dried fennel
  seeds
1 small shoulder of veal, boned
15 ml (1 tablespoon) flour
275 ml (½ pint) chicken stock

1 Grate the rind of the lemon, and squeeze the juice.
2 Melt the Outline in a small saucepan. Stir in the lemon juice, grated rind and seasoning to taste.
3 Reserve half the lemon mixture, and combine the remainder with the stuffing mix, egg yolk, fennel seeds and seasoning to taste.
4 Lay the boned veal, skin side down, on a board and spread with the stuffing mixture. Roll up tightly and tie in 3 places with strong white thread.
5 Brush with reserved lemon mixture, place the smooth side down in a roasting tin and put in the oven at 180°C 350°F, Gas 4, for 2 hours. Remove from tin and place on a warm serving dish. Remove thread.
6 Sprinkle the flour into the roasting tin, stir well, add the stock and continue stirring over moderate heat until thickened and smooth.
7 Serve each person with 100 g (4 oz) sliced stuffed veal, fresh fennel bulb and lettuce salad and 75 g (3 oz) tiny boiled potatoes.

SERVES 8   Calories per portion with vegetables 335 (365)

44

Turkey Escalopes with Mint

(See photograph pages 38–39)

4 x 100 g (4 oz) slices turkey
  breast
15 ml (1 tablespoon) seasoned
  flour
50 g (2 oz) Outline
150 ml (¼ pint) chicken stock
5 ml (1 teaspoon) vinegar

15 ml (1 tablespoon) mint jelly
100 g (4 oz) ribbon noodles,
  cooked
Sprigs of mint ⎫
Chopped chives ⎭ to garnish

1   Beat out the turkey breast slices as flat as possible and lightly dust with seasoned flour.
2   Melt half the Outline and use to sauté the turkey escalopes, two at a time, until golden brown on both sides. Add more Outline as necessary, but reserve 15 g (½ oz) Outline for the pasta. Remove from the pan and keep hot.
3   Add the stock, vinegar and mint jelly to the juices remaining in the pan and stir over heat until the jelly has melted.
4   Toss ribbon noodles with the remaining Outline and arrange on a warm serving dish. Place the escalopes, overlapping, on the pasta and spoon over the sauce. Garnish with sprigs of fresh mint and chopped chives.

SERVES 4 Calories per portion 345 (380)

Barbecued Pork Pockets

(See photograph pages 38–39)

4 x 150 g (5 oz) lean pork chops
1 small onion, finely chopped
5 ml (1 teaspoon) curry powder
Salt and pepper
60 ml (4 tablespoons) apple juice
30 ml (2 tablespoons) vinegar

5 ml (1 teaspoon) brown sugar
5 ml (1 teaspoon) ground
  cinnamon
5 ml (1 teaspoon) ground cloves

1   Trim fat from chops, dice and render out in a frying pan.
2   Using a sharp pointed knife slit the meat down to the bone to make pockets. Combine the onion and curry powder and use to fill the pockets. Season the chops on both sides.

3   Add the apple juice, vinegar, sugar, cinnamon and cloves to the rendered fat and stir well.
4   Brush chops on both sides with the spice mixture. Place on a rack and cook under a moderately hot grill for about 10 minutes on each side, basting with the spice mixture, until cooked and golden brown.
5   With each chop serve 100 g (4 oz) boiled new potatoes, with 15 g (½ oz) Outline melted and poured over all 4 portions, and a green salad.

SERVES 4

Calories per portion with potatoes and salad 410 (420)

Kitchen Garden Curry

25 g (1 oz) Outline
15 ml (1 tablespoon) ground coriander
7.5 ml (1½ teaspoons) chilli powder
5 ml (1 teaspoon) turmeric
5 ml (1 teaspoon) ground ginger
2.5 ml (½ teaspoon) powdered mustard
1 large onion, peeled and diced

25 g (1 oz) desiccated coconut infused for 1 hour in 725 ml (1¼ pints) beef stock
1 clove garlic, crushed
675 g (1½ lb) mixed fresh vegetables (carrots, celery, etc.)
56 g (2¾ oz) tomato purée
5 ml (1 teaspoon) lemon juice

1   Melt Outline in a medium-sized saucepan, add all the spices, onion and garlic.
2   Simmer for 5 minutes. Strain beef stock. Discard coconut.
3   Add remaining ingredients and cook until the vegetables are tender, 15–30 minutes depending on how crisp you like them.
4   Serve each portion with 125 g (4 oz) any lean meat.

SERVES 4

Calories per portion of curried vegetables 190 (195)
Calories per portion of curry with meat 400 (435)

Lemon Veal Kebabs

MARINADE

30 ml (2 tablespoons) oil
Juice of 1 lemon
Salt
Freshly ground black pepper
Onion salt
2.5 ml (½ teaspoon) oregano

KEBABS

350 g (12 oz) pie veal, trimmed
and cut into 2.5 cm (1 inch)
cubes
12 small button mushrooms,
washed

1 green pepper, blanched,
de-seeded and cut into 12
pieces
4 small, firm tomatoes, halved

LEMON SAUCE

1 quantity All-in-One coating
sauce (see basic recipe, page
11)
Salt and pepper
Grated rind of ½ lemon
Juice of 1 lemon

RICE

150 g (5 oz) rice

1 Mix together all the marinade ingredients. Put veal in a
   shallow dish, pour marinade over. Cover and refrigerate
   for 2–3 hours, turning occasionally.
2 Arrange veal, mushrooms, pepper and tomatoes on 4 long
   or 8 short kebab skewers.
3 Brush with marinade and place under a pre-heated
   medium-hot grill for 10–12 minutes, turning and brushing
   with marinade regularly.
4 Make up Lemon Sauce. Cook rice in boiling salted water
   10-15 minutes. Drain.
5 Serve kebabs on a bed of boiled rice with the Lemon Sauce
   handed separately.

SERVES 4 Calories per portion with sauce and rice 420 (430)

Fruity Rabbit Casserole

25 g (1 oz) Outline
4 x 250 g (9 oz) rabbit joints
1 large onion, sliced
25 g (1 oz) cornflour
1 orange, peeled and sliced

2 peppers, de-seeded and sliced
575 ml (1 pint) beef stock
Salt and pepper
2 sticks celery, chopped

1   Melt the Outline gently and lightly brown the rabbit joints
    for about 5 minutes.
2   Transfer the joints to a large casserole. Fry the onion for 5
    minutes.
3   Add remaining ingredients, bring to the boil, stirring
    continuously and pour over the rabbit joints in the cas-
    serole.
4   Cook covered in the centre of a pre-heated oven 160°C
    325°F, Gas 3, for 2–2½ hours.
5   Serve each portion with 100 g (4 oz) runner beans and 50 g
    (2 oz) sweetcorn.

SERVES 4   Calories per portion with vegetables 460 (475)

Lamb in Caper Sauce

4 large loin of lamb chops
Salt and pepper
15 g (½ oz) Outline
30 ml (2 tablespoons) chopped
    spring onion
275 ml (½ pint) All-in-One

coating sauce (see basic recipe
    page 11)
15 ml (1 tablespoon) capers
15 ml (1 tablespoon) lemon juice
60 ml (4 tablespoons) natural
    yogurt

1   Melt Outline in a frying pan and gently fry the chops for 5
    minutes on each side or until golden brown and cooked
    through.
2   Remove from the pan and keep hot.

3   Add the spring onion to the fat remaining in the pan and fry gently until golden. Drain and spoon over the chops.
4   Make the coating sauce, stir in capers, lemon juice and yogurt. Reheat and season to taste. Spoon the caper sauce over the chops.
5   Serve each person with one chop, sauce and 100 g (4 oz) minted peas.

SERVES 4   Calories per portion with vegetables 405 (420)

Easy Paella

25 g (1 oz) Outline
1 small onion, chopped
1 clove garlic, crushed
350 g (12 oz) cooked chicken, cubed
575 ml (1 pint) chicken stock
175 g (6 oz) long grain rice
100 g (4 oz) pimento, diced

3 tomatoes, skinned and quartered
2.5 ml (½ teaspoon) turmeric
5 ml (1 teaspoon) salt
2.5 ml (½ teaspoon) pepper
100 g (4 oz) shelled prawns
100 g (4 oz) shelled mussels
50 g (2 oz) frozen peas

1   Melt the Outline over low heat and gently fry the onion, garlic and chicken for 5 minutes.
2   Add remaining ingredients except the prawns, mussels and peas.
3   Cover and simmer for 30 minutes. Five minutes before the end of the cooking time, stir in the remaining ingredients. Cover and complete the cooking time.
4   Serve each portion with 75 g (3 oz) green beans.

SERVES 4   Calories per portion 400 (400)

Light Meals

Chunky Veal Soup

(See photograph page 37)

25 g (1 oz) Outline
450 g (1 lb) lean veal, cut into
  small cubes
1 medium onion, chopped
400 g (14 oz) can tomatoes

Salt and pepper
Bouquet garni
575 ml (1 pint) chicken stock
100 g (4 oz) pasta spirals

1   Melt the Outline and fry the veal and onion (5 minutes).
2   Stir in remaining ingredients except the pasta spirals.
    Bring to the boil, cover and simmer for 20 minutes.
3   Stir in the pasta spirals and cook for a further 15 minutes or
    until the pasta is cooked.

SERVES 4   Calories per portion 280 (295)

Tomato and Tuna Jelly

(See photograph page 37)

1 lemon-flavoured packet jelly
275 ml (½ pint) hot water
275 ml (½ pint) cider vinegar
6 large tomatoes, sliced
100 g (4 oz) mixed cooked
  vegetables – peas, carrots,

sweetcorn, beans, etc.
99 g (3½ oz) can tuna fish,
  drained and flaked
Watercress

1   Dissolve jelly in the hot water and make up to 575 ml
    (1 pint) with cider vinegar. Cool.
2   Put a layer of sliced tomatoes in the bottom of a wetted
    1 litre (2 pint) ring mould or 4 individual moulds.
3   Pour over a little of the cooled jelly mixture and allow to
    set in the refrigerator or cool larder before adding alternate
    layers of vegetables, tuna fish and more tomatoes.

4   Pour remaining jelly over carefully and allow to set.
5   Unmould onto a serving dish and fill centre with water-
    cress, or turn out individual moulds on to small plates and
    garnish.

This can be served as a first course, on its own or to accompany
cold meat.

SERVES 4   Calories per portion 175 (175)

Herbed Cucumber Omelettes

(See photograph page 37)

FILLING

½ cucumber, diced
5 ml (1 teaspoon) salt
15 g (½ oz) Outline
15 ml (1 tablespoon) chopped
  fresh herbs such as parsley,
  mint, thyme and marjoram

OMELETTES

8 eggs
Salt and pepper
25 g (1 oz) Outline for frying

1   Make the filling. Sprinkle the cucumber dice with salt and
    allow to stand for 30 minutes. Drain off the juices.
2   Melt the Outline in a frying pan. Add the cucumber dice
    and sauté over moderate heat for 2 minutes. Sprinkle over
    the herbs and continue cooking for 1 further minute. Keep
    warm while you make the four 2-egg omelettes.
3   Whisk up 2 eggs with 1 teaspoon cold water and seasoning
    to taste. Melt a quarter of the Outline in an omelette pan
    and pour in the egg mixture. Cook and stir over moderate
    heat until lightly set. Spoon one quarter of the cucumber
    mixture into the cooked omelette, and fold over on to a
    warm plate.
4   Repeat with the remaining ingredients, to make 4 omelet-
    tes in all. If liked, sprinkle the folded omelettes with more
    chopped herbs.
5   Serve each omelette with 2 fingers of toasted wholemeal
    bread spread with Outline.

SERVES 4   Calories per portion with toast 290 (290)

Desserts

Red and Black Currant Ice

(See photograph page 40)

350 g (12 oz) red and black
    currants
575 ml (1 pint) water
Artificial liquid sweetener
    equivalent to 225 g (8 oz)

sugar, according to
    manufacturer's instructions
Rind and juice of 1 lemon
2 egg whites

1   Top and tail the red and black currants.
2   Simmer together the fruit, water, sweetener, lemon rind.
    Leave to cool.
3   Add the lemon juice and pour into an ice-cube tray.
4   Half freeze, then empty into a bowl, whisk the egg whites
    and stir into the fruit mixture.
5   Re-freeze.

SERVES 4   Calories per portion 45 (45)

Peach and Strawberry Fluff

(See photograph page 40)

1 strawberry flavour packet jelly
275 ml (½ pint) boiling water
Few drops almond essence
350 g (12 oz) strawberries

2 ripe peaches
1 egg white

1   Make up the jelly with the boiling water, add almond
    essence to taste and allow to cool.
2   Hull all the strawberries and reserve a few for decoration.
    Halve the rest
3   When the jelly is syrupy, peel the peaches, halve them,
    remove the stones and slice.
4   Whisk the jelly until foamy and doubled in bulk. Fold in
    the peach slices and halved strawberries.

5   Stiffly wisk the egg white and fold lightly into the fruit and jelly mixture.
6   Spoon into short-stemmed wine glasses and allow to set.
7   Serve decorated with the reserved strawberries.

SERVES 4 Calories per portion 145 (145)

Gooseberry Mint Snow

(See photograph page 40)

450 g (1 lb) ripe gooseberries
100 g (4 oz) sugar
Granulated sweetener equivalent
   to 100 g (4 oz) sugar according
   to manufacturer's instructions
4 large sprigs mint

1 egg yolk
Few drops peppermint essence
Few drops green food colouring
Artificial liquid sweetener (if
   required)
2 egg whites

1   Top and tail the gooseberries and place them in a saucepan with just sufficient water to cover, the sweetener and a few leaves from each sprig of mint.
2   Cover and stew gently for about 20 minutes, or until soft. Press through a sieve. Return to the rinsed out saucepan.
3   Reheat to boiling point, remove from the heat, and beat in the egg yolk. Add the peppermint essence and food colouring, and the liquid sweetener if required.
4   Whisk the egg whites until stiff and fold into the purée. Spoon into 4 sundae glasses and allow to set.
5   Serve decorated with tiny sprigs of mint.

SERVES 4 Calories per portion 75 (95)

Black Cherry Gateau

(See photograph page 40)

1 quantity Victoria Sandwich
  Cake mixture (see basic recipe
  page 13), adding grated rind
  of 1 orange to ingredients
  before mixing.

FILLING

30 ml (2 tablespoons) natural
  low-fat yogurt

5 ml (1 teaspoon) artificial
  sweetener, to taste
100 g (4 oz) curd cheese
50 g (2 oz) black cherries, sliced
1 lemon, segmented
Icing sugar to dredge
Black cherries to decorate

1   Prepare and bake cakes.
2   Turn out and cool on a wire tray.
3   Mix all the filling ingredients together.
4   Sandwich the cakes together with the filling mixture.
5   Dredge with icing sugar and decorate with black cherries.

Calories for whole cake 2460 (2425)
Calories for ⅛th of cake 310 (305)

Chocolate Fairy Cakes

1 quantity chocolate Victoria
  Sandwich Cake mixture (see
  basic recipe page 13)

150 ml (¼ pint) Creamy
  Topping (see recipe page 32)
24 blanched almonds

1   Divide the mixture between 24 paper bun cases standing in
    bun tins or on a baking sheet. Bake in oven at 190°C 375°F
    Gas 5 for 15–20 minutes. until well risen and firm to the
    touch.
2   Cool. Cut off a small slice of each cake. Pipe in a rosette of
    Creamy Topping (see recipe page 32) and decorate with an
    almond and the sliced off 'lid' of cake.

Calories per cake 105 (100)

Summer Ideas

1 Keep the garden weeds at bay but remember to bend your knees, not your back, while doing it. If you use a hoe, straighten your back twice a minute, which will turn this useful job into an excellent exercise.
2 Persuade the family or friends to go with you on a picking expedition to a local fruit farm. It is worth quite a long drive if necessary. Have the fun of picking your own fruit, saving money, and as fruit is relatively low in energy, you can sample as you pick.
3 If the sun does not suit you, or you have a problem keeping cool in hot weather, organise your life to avoid getting overheated. Move slowly but steadily, keep on the shady side of the street, do your shopping in the morning or evening and keep your anti-perspirant and talcum powder handy. Remember, the fatter you are the warmer you may feel.
4 Dark colours are frequently more flattering to an over-weight figure than light ones. Navy looks cool in the summer; keep any stripes vertical and don't draw attention to your lack of waistline by wearing a contrasting white belt.

Summer Drinks

SUMMER PUNCH

Sieve 100 g (4 oz) strawberries or raspberries and mix the juice with liquid sweetener to taste and 275 ml (½ pint) slimmers' tonic water. Pour over ice cubes and drink through a straw.

LEMON GINGER

Strain the juice of half a lemon into a tall glass and add liquid sweetener to taste. Pour in slimmers' ginger ale to fill the glass and float a twist of lemon on top.

Autumn

The warm autumn weather makes a perfect time to launch your beautifying, health-giving diet, trim up with exercises and present a pretty figure for the forthcoming party season. Now is the time to sign up for evening classes. Keep fit and yoga classes are very popular and both are recommended for slimmers. Give yourself the confidence to wear your most revealing dress and don't forget that a healthy slimming diet gives you a glowing complexion and glossy hair. There's a harvest festival all autumn long with fruit and vegetables aplenty for slimmers. What could make better eating than the exciting recipes given here for sun-ripened melon, grapes and tomatoes; or exotic aubergines and peppers? With all the incentive autumn brings to a dieter, it should be delightfully easy to lose just the amount of weight you desire.

Clockwise from the front, Super Celery Salad, Crispy Stuffed Tomatoes, Greek Cheese Salad and Cheesey Melon Wedges

Marinated Lamb Skewers, Grape
Salad with Toasted Coconut,
Orange Parsley Chicken, Blackberry
Baked Apples

Autumn Specials

BREAKFAST IDEAS (All around 200 Calories)

1 Soak 50 g (2 oz) dried apricots in 100 ml (4 fl oz) strong black tea overnight. Add artificial sweetener to taste and serve sprinkled with 15 ml (1 tablespoon) toasted unsweetened breakfast cereal.
2 Two well-grilled chipolata sausages and 2 tomatoes and 4 mushrooms dotted with Outline and grilled.
3 100 g (4 oz) portion of a smoked kipper and 1 tomato dotted with Outline and grilled.
4 Two small slices of slimmers' bread and 100 g (4 oz) mushrooms sautéed in 6 g (¼ oz) Outline and 15 ml (1 tablespoon) water.
5 One small banana and 1 apple and 25 g (1 oz) Edam cheese.

NIBBLES

All these can be taken in addition to your daily diet, but don't make a meal of them.

1 A nibble bowl of crisp vegetable bites to prepare and keep in an airtight container in the refrigerator: carrot sticks, tomato wedges, pepper strips, sliced fennel, shredded Brussels sprouts.
2 Raw mushrooms with mild onion rings and garlic salt.
3 Seasoned tomato juice set with gelatine.
4 Half a small apple, thinly sliced.
5 15 ml (1 tablespoon) cottage cheese mixed with an equal quantity of chopped pear or plum.

Top left, Pipérade with Eggs

Top right, Pizza Deliziosa

Centre left, Fish Knots

Centre right, Beef Sausages with Cranberry Glaze

Bottom left, Crispy-Topped Marrow

Bottom right, Harlequin Chicken Salad

Starters

Cheesey Melon Wedges

(See photograph page 57)

4 x 175 g (6 oz) slices of
   cantaloupe melon
227 g (8 oz) cottage cheese
Salt and pepper

5 ml (1 teaspoon) mixed herbs
175 g (6 oz) lean ham, diced
Chopped chives to garnish

1   Score the melon flesh as in photograph page 57.
2   Mix together the cheese, seasoning, herbs and ham.
3   Pile onto the melon wedges and garnish with chopped chives.

SERVES 4   Calories per portion 185 (180)

Greek Cheese Salad

(See photograph page 57)

1 lettuce
12 black olives
100 g (4 oz) fetta cheese or 175 g
   (6 oz) cottage cheese
2 medium tomatoes

1 slice white bread
25 g (1 oz) Outline
15 ml (1 tablespoon) lemon juice
Salt and black pepper

1   Remove outer leaves of lettuce and tear up the inner leaves into small pieces.
2   Halve and stone the olives. Crumble up the fetta cheese. (This is not necessary if you are using cottage cheese.) Peel the tomatoes, remove the seeds and chop the flesh roughly.

3   Trim crusts from the bread and cut into small dice. Melt the Outline in a frying pan and gently fry the bread dice until crisp and golden brown.
4   Carefully combine the cheese, olives, tomato, fried bread dice, and lemon juice. Season the mixture well.
5   Divide the lettuce pieces between individual salad bowls and top with the cheese salad mixture.

SERVES 4   Calories per portion 95 (105)

Super Celery Salad

(See photograph page 57)

5 ml (1 teaspoon) yeast extract
10 ml (2 teaspoons) tomato purée
5 ml (1 teaspoon) sugar
150 ml (¼ pint) beef stock
1 head of celery

25 g (1 oz) Outline
60 ml (4 tablespoons) soured cream
Paprika pepper

1   Disssolve the yeast extract, tomato purée and sugar in the stock.
2   Trim the celery and divide into 4 portions. Trim each quarter to a 15 cm (6 inch) length and cook the trimmings in the stock for use in a soup.
3   Put the celery quarters side by side in a shallow baking dish and pour over the strained stock. Dot with the Outline.
4   Cover with foil and cook at 190°C 375°F, Gas 5, for 30–40 minutes, or until the celery is tender. Turn the quarters over halfway through cooking time. Cool in the liquid.
5   Using a slotted draining spoon place a celery quarter on each serving plate.
6   Beat the remaining juices in the baking dish with the soured cream and spoon over the celery. Dust the tops with paprika. Chill before serving.

SERVES 4   Calories per portion 65 (65)

Crispy Stuffed Tomatoes

(See photograph page 57)

4 large tomatoes
1 crisp eating apple, cored and diced
10 ml (2 teaspoons) lemon juice
75 g (3 oz) Edam cheese, diced
3 pickled gherkins, chopped
25 g (1 oz) walnuts, roughly chopped

5 ml (1 teaspoon) chopped chives
15 ml (1 tablespoon) slimmers' salad dressing
Salt and pepper
Lettuce leaves
Watercress to garnish

1   Cut tops off tomatoes and scoop out the seeds.
2   Combine apple and lemon juice, to prevent apple turning brown. Add cheese, gherkins, walnuts and chives.
3   Add salad dressing to bind. Season with salt and pepper.
4   Fill the tomato cases with the stuffing and replace tops.
5   Arrange on a bed of lettuce and garnish with watercress.

SERVES 4   Calories per portion 135 (145)

Stuffed Peppers

25 g (1 oz) Outline
100 g (4 oz) cooked chicken, diced
100 g (4 oz) mushrooms, finely chopped
283 g (10 oz) can bean shoots
1 onion, peeled and chopped

15 ml (1 tablespoon) soy sauce
Salt and pepper
2 large green peppers, halved lengthwise, de-seeded and blanched
20 ml (4 teaspoons) low-fat natural yogurt

1   Melt Outline gently in a frying pan. Add chicken, mushrooms, drained bean shoots, onion, soy sauce and seasoning. Sauté over a low heat for 10 minutes.
2   Place halved peppers in an ovenproof dish greased with a little Outline. Fill with prepared chicken and mushroom.
3   Cover dish with greased aluminium foil. Bake in preheated oven 180°C 350°F, Gas 4, for 40-50 minutes.
4   Serve hot or cold, topping with 5 ml (1 teaspoon) yogurt.

SERVES 4   Calories per portion 100 (110)

Main Meals

Marinated Lamb Skewers

(See photograph pages 58–59)

MARINADE

50 g (2 oz) Outline
30 ml (2 tablespoons) lemon
   juice
15 ml (1 tablespoon) tomato
   purée
Salt and black pepper

350 g (12 oz) boned lean lamb
8 small bay leaves
12 small onions, quartered

100 g (4 oz) button mushrooms
8 chunks canned pineapple

TURMERIC RICE

175 g (6 oz) long grain rice
25 g (1 oz) Outline
5 ml (1 teaspoon) ground
   turmeric
5 ml (1 teaspoon) grated lemon
   rind

1   Make the marinade. Melt Outline gently in a saucepan.
     Stir in the lemon juice, tomato purée and salt and pepper to
     taste.
2   Cut the lamb into neat cubes. Remove the saucepan from
     the heat, add the lamb cubes, and stir until they are just
     coated in the hot marinade. Cover and allow to stand for
     1 hour.
3   Thread 4 long skewers with alternate cubes of meat, bay
     leaves, onions, mushrooms and pineapple. Brush with the
     remaining marinade. Grill under moderate heat, turning
     occasionally, for about 15 minutes, or until the meat is
     tender.
4   Meanwhile, cook the rice in plenty of boiling salted water
     for about 14 minutes. Drain well. Rinse the saucepan, melt
     the Outline in it, stir in the turmeric and lemon rind, then
     carefully fold in the cooked rice.
5   Serve each skewer on a bed of turmeric rice.

SERVES 4   Calories per portion 555 (560)

Orange Parsley Chicken

(See photograph pages 58–59)

2 large oranges
50 g (2 oz) Outline
30 ml (2 tablespoons) chopped parsley
Salt and pepper
227 g (8 oz) cooked or canned sweetcorn kernels

50 g (2 oz) parsley and thyme stuffing mix
1 egg yolk
1 small roasting chicken
Parsley sprigs to garnish

1   Cut the oranges in half and squeeze out the juice. Carefully scoop out the pith and reserve the cups.
2   Melt the Outline and combine with the parsley and orange juice. Season to taste.
3   Stir half the corn into the stuffing mix with 90 ml (6 tablespoons) of the orange juice mixture and the egg yolk. Use to stuff the chicken.
4   Roast the chicken at 190°C 375°F, Gas 5, for approximately 1½ hours, basting frequently with the orange parsley mixture, until golden brown and the juices are clear when tested with a fork.
5   Serve the roast chicken portions with orange cups filled with hot corn, and garnished with parsley sprigs.

SERVES 4   Calories per portion 320 (340)

Hawaiian Gammon Rashers

4 x 100 g (4 oz) lean gammon rashers
15 g (½ oz) Outline
5 ml (1 teaspoon) French mustard

4 slices of pineapple in natural juices
142 g (5 fl oz) low-fat natural yogurt
½ bunch watercress

1   Trim gammon rashers, removing any visible fat.
2   Mix Outline and mustard together and spread each gammon rasher with a little of this mixture.

3   Place under a pre-heated grill, turning once until cooked (15–20 minutes). Top each rasher with a pineapple ring and re-heat for 2–3 minutes. Arrange in a serving dish.

4   Reserve a few sprigs of watercress as garnish. Finely chop the rest and mix with yogurt. Place a little on top of each gammon rasher. Garnish with sprigs of watercress.

SERVES 4   Calories per portion 270 (275)

Apple Curry Sauce on Baked Ham

25 g (1 oz) Outline
4 x 100 (4 oz) ham steaks
1 medium onion, chopped
15 ml (1 tablespoon) curry
  powder
Salt

2 large cooking apples
30 ml (2 tablespoons) boiling
  water
15 ml (1 tablespoon) flaked
  almonds

1   Use a little Outline to grease a shallow baking dish. Arrange the ham steaks in it and bake in the oven at 190°C 375°F, Gas 5, for 15 minutes.

2   Meanwhile, cook the onion in the remaining Outline until soft but not coloured. Stir in the curry powder and a little salt.

3   Peel, core and slice the apples, add to the onion and stir well. Cover and cook gently for about 10 minutes, or until soft. Beat until smooth with the boiling water. Taste and add more salt if necessary.

4   Spoon the sauce over the ham steaks, sprinkle with the almonds and return to the oven for a further 10 minutes.

5   Serve each person with a ham steak and sauce, and 100 g (4 oz) cooked cauliflower florets sprinkled with chopped parsley.

SERVES 4   Calories per portion with vegetables 290 (330)

Chicken and Cucumber

SAUCE

25 g (1 oz) Outline
25 g (1 oz) flour, plain
425 ml (¾ pint) chicken stock,
  using one stock cube

100 g (4 oz) rice
100 g (4 oz) peas, cooked

1 small can pimentos, drained
  and sliced

450 g (1 lb) cooked chicken,
  chopped
½ cucumber, diced
Salt and pepper

1 Make sauce (see page 11) using chicken stock instead of
   milk. Add the chicken and cucumber, seasoned to taste,
   and reheat.
2 Cook rice in boiling salted water for 10–15 minutes. Drain.
   Add peas and pimentos and reheat.
3 Serve chicken and cucumber on bed of rice mixture.

SERVES 4 Calories per portion 360 (380)

Piquant Fish

MARINADE

2 x 142 g (5 oz) cartons of
  low-fat natural yogurt
30 ml (2 tablespoons) lemon
  juice
5 ml (1 teaspoon) chilli powder
1 clove garlic, crushed

Salt and pepper
Pinch of ginger

4 x 175 g (6 oz) portions of
  white fish
25 g (1 oz) Outline, melted
175 g (6 oz) long grain rice

1 Mix all marinade ingredients together and pour over the
   fish.
2 Cover and leave in refrigerator or cool larder for 2–3
   hours, turning occasionally.
3 Place the fish on grill pan and brush with the melted
   Outline. Grill for 5–7 minutes on each side until cooked.
4 Cook the rice in boiling salted water for 10–15 minutes,
   drain.
5 Heat the remaining marinade and serve with the fish.

SERVES 4 Calories per portion 400 (400)

Light Meals

Harlequin Chicken Salad

(See photograph page 60)

350 g (12 oz) cooked chicken, cut
  into small pieces
¼ cucumber, diced
1 medium-sized onion, peeled
  and diced
1 green pepper, de-seeded and
  diced
4 sticks celery, diced

DRESSING
75 g (3 oz) low-fat natural
  yogurt
Juice of 1 lemon
Salt and ground black pepper
Paprika pepper
Lettuce leaves

1   Combine chicken and vegetables.
2   Mix the yogurt, lemon juice and seasoning together.
3   Toss chicken and vegetables in dressing until completely
    covered.
4   Serve on a bed of lettuce leaves.

SERVES 4   Calories per portion 185 (180)

Fish Knots

(See photograph page 60)

4 x 100 g (4 oz) fillets plaice or
  any white fish
Seasoned flour
1 egg
15 ml (1 tablespoon) water

50 g (2 oz) dry breadcrumbs
75 g (3 oz) Outline, melted
Onion salt and pepper
2.5 ml (½ teaspoon) dried dill
Lemon wedges to garnish

1   Cut the fish into very narrow strips about 12 cm (5 inches)
    long and dust lightly with seasoned flour. Tie each strip in
    a single knot.
2   Beat the egg with the water and use to coat the fish knots.
    Roll in the breadcrumbs.

69

3   Well grease a baking sheet with melted Outline. Arrange the knots on it and sprinkle with onion salt, pepper and dried dill. Drizzle the remaining Outline over them.
4   Bake at 200°C 400°F, Gas 6, for 15 minutes, or until golden brown and crisp.
5   Serve each person with a portion of the fish knots garnished with lemon wedges and accompanied by a sliced cucumber salad.

SERVES 4 Calories per portion 210 (230)

Pipérade with Eggs

(See photograph page 60)

75 g (3 oz) Outline
1 large onion, sliced
1 medium green pepper,
  de-seeded and sliced
1 medium red pepper, de-seeded
  and sliced

4 medium tomatoes, sliced
5 ml (1 teaspoon) dried thyme
Salt and pepper
4 eggs
15 ml (1 tablespoon) oil
4 small slices slimmers' bread

1   Melt two-thirds of the Outline in a deep frying pan. Add the onion, pepper and tomato slices, thyme and seasoning to taste. Cover and cook gently without browning for 10 minutes or until soft.
2   Make 4 hollows with the back of a spoon in the mixture and break 1 egg into each. Cover and cook gently until set.
3   Meanwhile, in a shallow frying pan heat the remaining Outline and the oil. Trim the bread slices and cut each into 2 triangles. Fry all 8 triangles together in the fat until golden brown. Sprinkle with a little seasoning.
4   Serve each person with a portion of pipérade topped with an egg, garnished with 2 croutons.

SERVES 4 Calories per portion with croutons 265 (275)

Pizza Delíziosa

(See photograph page 60)

SCONE BASE

25 g (1 oz) Outline
100 g (4 oz) self-raising flour
2.5 ml (½ teaspoon) baking
  powder
2.5 ml (½ teaspoon) salt
2.5 ml (½ teaspoon) mixed
  herbs
1 standard egg
15 ml (1 tablespoon) skimmed
  milk

TOPPING

15 g (½ oz) Outline
1 small onion, chopped
100 g (4 oz) mushrooms,
  chopped
184 g (6½ oz) can tomatoes
Salt and pepper
5 ml (1 teaspoon) oregano
50 g (2 oz) garlic sausage
75 g (3 oz) Edam cheese, grated
4 anchovies, halved
25 g (1 oz) black olives, halved
  and stoned

1 Sieve flour, baking powder and salt into a mixing bowl.
   Add remaining scone ingredients. Mix with a wooden
   spoon to form a soft dough.
2 Knead lightly on a floured worktop.
3 Place dough on a baking sheet and with lightly floured
   fingers form into a 25 cm (10 inch) round.
4 Melt the Outline and gently fry the onion (5 minutes).
   Add the mushrooms and cook a further 3 minutes.
5 Stir in the tomatoes, seasoning and oregano.
6 Spread over the scone base.
7 Top with the slices of sausage and sprinkle over the cheese.
   Decorate with anchovies and black olives.
8 Bake on the second from top shelf of a pre-heated oven
   200°C 400°F, Gas 6, for 25 minutes.

SERVES 4 Calories per portion 280 (305)

71

Beef Sausages with Cranberry Glaze

(See photograph page 60)

12 beef chipolata sausages
25 g (1 oz) Outline
Pinch of ground ginger
5 ml (1 teaspoon) grated orange
    rind

30 ml (2 tablespoons) orange
    juice
45 ml (3 tablespoons) cranberry
    jelly
4 medium tomatoes, sliced
Parsley to garnish

1   Grill the sausages until cooked through and brown.
2   Meanwhile, melt half the Outline in a saucepan and add
    the ginger, orange rind, orange juice and jelly. Stir until
    well blended and bring to the boil. Simmer for 5 minutes.
3   Place tomato slices on a heat-proof plate. Melt the remaining
    Outline and drizzle over them. Grill for 3 minutes.
4   Arrange the sausages on the tomatoes and spoon the sauce
    over them. Return to the grill for 3–5 minutes until the
    glaze is bubbly. Garnish with sprigs of parsley.
5   Serve each person with 3 glazed sausages and a portion of
    the tomatoes.

SERVES 4   Calories per portion 420 (425)

Crispy-Topped Marrow

(See photograph page 60)

1 medium marrow
90 ml (6 tablespoons) water
75 g (3 oz) Outline
15 ml (1 tablespoon)
    chopped fresh herbs, tarragon,
    parsley, thyme

100 g (4 oz) lean minced beef
100 g (4 oz) mushrooms,
    chopped
1 small onion, grated
50 g (2 oz) Edam cheese, grated
25 g (1 oz) toasted breadcrumbs

1   Peel the marrow, de-seed and cut into large dice.
2   Place the water and one third of the Outline in a saucepan
    and heat until the Outline melts. Add the marrow dice and
    seasoning to taste. Bring to the boil, cover and cook gently
    for 10 minutes, turning once. Drain and stir in the herbs.
3   Meanwhile, form the mince, mushroom and onion into
    small balls and brown in another one third of the Outline
    for about 10 minutes.

4   Place the marrow in an ovenproof casserole, cover with the meat balls. Mix together the cheese and breadcrumbs and sprinkle over these. Dot with the rest of the Outline.
5   Bake at 200°C 400°F Gas 6 for 20–25 minutes.

SERVES 4   Calories per portion 215 (235)

Desserts

Blackberry Baked Apples

(See photograph pages 58–59)

4 x 175 g (6 oz) baking apples,
*   cored*
4 slices slimmers' bread, crumbed
Rind and juice of 1 orange

Pinch of cinnamon
100 g (4 oz) blackberries
Artificial liquid sweetener

1   Score apple skins round middle.
2   Mix together remaining ingredients, and use to fill cavities of apples.
3   Wrap each apple in foil and place on a baking sheet.
4   Bake in the centre of a pre-heated oven, 190°C 375°F, Gas 5, for 30–40 minutes.

SERVES 4   Calories per portion 115 (115)

Grape Salad with Toasted Coconut

(See photograph pages 58–59)

225 g (8 oz) white grapes
225 g (8 oz) black grapes
4 small dessert apples
150 ml (¼ pint) unsweetened
  orange juice

Few drops artificial liquid
  sweetener (if required)
15 g (½ oz) Outline
25 g (1 oz) shredded coconut

1   Halve the grapes and remove the seeds. Core and thinly
    slice the apples, without removing peel.
2   Place all the fruit in a glass dish and pour over the orange
    juice. Add a few drops of artificial sweetener if required.
3   Melt the Outline in a small saucepan, stir in the shredded
    coconut. Spread out on a sheet of foil in a grill pan and
    toast under a hot grill until golden.
4   Serve the salad sprinkled with the toasted coconut.

SERVES 4   Calories per portion 155 (160)

Plum and Rhubarb with Hazelnut Crust

4 large ripe plums
225 g (8 oz) rhubarb, trimmed
60 ml (4 tablespoons) water
Artificial liquid sweetener
50 g (2 oz) plain flour
1.25 ml (¼ teaspoon) cinnamon

25 g (1 oz) Outline
25 g (1 oz) chopped toasted
  hazelnuts
15 ml (1 tablespoon) demerara
  sugar

1   Stone the plums and cut rhubarb into short lengths. Stew
    together in the water for about 5 minutes or until just
    tender. Sweeten to taste. Turn into a shallow ovenproof
    dish.
2   Sift the flour and cinnamon into a bowl. Rub in the Out-
    line and stir in the hazelnuts. Spoon over the fruit mixture
    and sprinkle with sugar.
3   Bake in the oven at 190°C 375°F, Gas 5, for 20 minutes,
    until the topping is crisp.

SERVES 4   Calories per portion 130 (150)

Autumn Ideas

1 Home-made tomato juice, delicately seasoned, is delicious and non-fattening. Use a lemon squeezer to rub the pulp off the skins, then sieve out the seeds. Add the seasoning of your choice; seasoned pepper, garlic salt, lemon juice, Worcestershire sauce.

2 While the weather is still mild, take up garden plants which would not survive the winter out of doors, and divide the hardier perennials. Autumn is tidying-up time and raking leaves together for the bonfire is fun as well as good exercise.

3 Buy plenty of apples and pears while the prices are low. They store well in trays, each piece of fruit separately wrapped in soft paper.

4 Make a personal effort to collect the hedgerow harvest of blackberries. Wear thin gloves to avoid staining your fingers or pricking them badly. Wash and eat the blackberries sprinkled with liquid sweetener, or stew them and sweeten the same way.

Autumn Drinks

BLENDER COCKTAIL (Serves 1)

Put 4 thin slices peeled cucumber in the blender with 60 ml (4 tablespoons) tomato juice, a few drops each of Worcestershire sauce and lemon juice and an ice cube. Cover and blend until smooth. Add extra salt to season if liked and serve in a stemmed glass decorated with a sprig of mint.

PEACH MILKSHAKE (Serves 1)

Sieve the flesh of a small ripe peach and combine with 150 ml (¼ pint) chilled skimmed milk and liquid sweetener to taste. Pour into a tall glass and add a swoosh of soda water.

Winter

This is a splendid season to slim since you are burning up plenty of energy just to keep yourself warm. A winter slimming programme can be much easier and more successful when the frost is on your window panes. Get your circulation going each day with morning exercises, or if you prefer the delicious comfort of a warm bedroom, do them at night. Take advantage of every crisp cold day to bring a glow to your cheeks by having a brisk walk. Come home to appetising hot soups, and the other hearty dishes suggested in the tempting recipes for this season. With carrots, red cabbage, and nutty Brussels sprouts available to choose from to go with the main course, you can even treat yourself to a small portion of steamed pudding as well. At parties remember to ask for sugar-free long drinks, make them last, and limit your nibbling to a minimum. Then you will be able to face the bathroom scales the morning after.

Clockwise from the front, Tomato and Celery Soup, Brussels Sprout Soup, Beefy Beetroot Soup and Golden Vegetable Soup

Clockwise from the front, Beef Olives with
Walnuts and Beansprouts, Curried Beef with
Bananas with side dishes, Green Pasta
Bolognaise and Chicken Portions with Fennel

Winter Specials

BREAKFAST IDEAS (Around 200 Calories)

All these can be taken with tea or coffee and skimmed milk.

1 Lemon mushrooms on toast: Melt 15 g (½ oz) Outline and add 5 ml (1 teaspoon) lemon juice. Use to sauté 100 g (4 oz) small button mushrooms until they are just cooked. Serve on 1 slice slimmers' bread thinly spread with Outline. Sprinkle with chopped parsley.

2 One orange and 1 standard egg, boiled, and 2 crispbreads thinly spread with Outline.

3 One egg poached and served on 1 slice of slimmers' bread toasted and thinly spread with Outline and 100 ml (4 fl oz) unsweetened orange juice.

4 Half a grapefruit and 1 slice of slimmers' bread thinly spread with Outline and 2 lamb's kidneys and 50 g (2 oz) mushrooms dotted with Outline and grilled.

5 Three small well-grilled rashers of streaky bacon with 45 ml (3 tablespoons) chopped and stewed fresh tomatoes and 1 crispbread.

NIBBLES

All these can be taken in addition to your daily diet allowance, but don't make a meal of them.

1 A nibble bowl of crisp vegetable bites to prepare and keep in an airtight container in the refrigerator: sprigs of watercress, cauliflower florets, matchstick lengths of celery, beetroot slices, shredded Chinese cabbage leaves and red cabbage.

2 15 ml (1 tablespoon) chopped pickled beetroot mixed with 5 ml (1 teaspoon) natural yogurt.

3 One crispbread thinly spread with meat or vegetable extract.

4 Half a grapefruit.

5 15 ml (1 tablespoon) cottage cheese mixed with thin rings of raw leek.

Moist Banana Tea Bread, Princess Pudding, Two-fruits
Pudding and Eve's Temptation Apples

Starters

Golden Vegetable Soup

(See photograph page 80)

100 g (4 oz) carrot
100 g (4 oz) parsnip
100 g (4 oz) swede
225 g (8 oz) leeks
2 sticks celery

25 g (1 oz) Outline
50 g (2 oz) red lentils
575 ml (1 pint) chicken stock
Salt and pepper

1   Peel and finely dice the root vegetables. Slice the leeks and chop the celery. Melt the Outline over low heat and gently fry the vegetables for 5 minutes.
2   Add lentils, stock and seasoning. Bring to the boil and simmer for 35–40 minutes.

SERVES 4   Calories per portion 105 (115)

Beefy Beetroot Soup

(See photograph page 80)

15 g (½ oz) Outline
1 small onion, grated
425 g (15 oz) can beef consommé
450 g (1 lb) diced cooked beetroot

Salt and pepper
15 ml (1 tablespoon) chopped
   parsley

1   Melt the Outline and use to cook the grated onion in a saucepan until soft but not brown, stirring all the time.
2   Add the consommé and bring to the boil. Add the beetroot, season, cover and simmer for 20 minutes.
3   Strain the soup into a measuring jug. Reserve 60 ml (4 tablespoons) diced beetroot for the garnish. Keep this warm, discarding the rest of the beetroot.

4 Make up soup to 575 ml (1 pint) with water if necessary. Taste and adjust seasoning. Return to the saucepan and reheat to boiling point.
5 Serve each person with a small cup of soup, garnished with 15 ml (1 tablespoon) beetroot dice and a little chopped parsley.

SERVES 4   Calories per portion 95 (100)

Brussels Sprout Soup

(See photograph page 80)

450 g (1 lb) Brussels sprouts	275 ml (½ pint) water
25 g (1 oz) Outline	275 ml (½ pint) skimmed milk
15 ml spoon (1 tablespoon) flour	Salt and black pepper
1 chicken stock cube	Pinch of ground nutmeg

1 Trim the sprouts and cook them in boiling salted water until tender. Drain and chop roughly.
2 Melt the Outline and stir in the flour; cook for 1 minute. Dissolve the stock cube in the water and skimmed milk. Add gradually to the flour and Outline mixture. Bring to the boil, stirring constantly.
3 Add the sprouts and cook gently for a further 10 minutes, stirring occasionally.
4 Liquidize or sieve and return to the rinsed–out saucepan. Season with salt, pepper and nutmeg, and reheat.

SERVES 4   Calories per portion 90 (90)

Tomato and Celery Soup

(See photograph page 77)

575 ml (1 pint) chicken stock
3 sticks celery, finely chopped
400 ml (14 fl oz) tomato juice
2 tomatoes, skinned, de-seeded
    and diced

10 ml (2 teaspoons)
    Worcestershire sauce
Rind and juice of 1 orange
5 ml (1 teaspoon) dried sweet
    basil

1   Place chicken stock and celery in a saucepan.
2   Bring to boil, cover, and simmer for 10 minutes.
3   Add remaining ingredients and continue simmering for a
    further 5 minutes.

    Serve immediately.

SERVES 4   Calories per portion 45 (45)

Main Meals

Chicken Portions with Fennel

(See photograph pages 78-79)

4 chicken portions, skinned
40 g (1½ oz) Outline, melted
Salt and pepper
5 ml (1 teaspoon) Worcestershire
    sauce

2 small heads fennel
1 medium onion, chopped
275 ml (½ pint) chicken stock
450 g (1 lb) mashed potato
15 ml (1 tablespoon) cornflour

1   Place the chicken portions, flesh side down, in a roasting
    tin greased with melted Outline. Season and bake in the
    oven at 190°C 375°F, Gas 5, for 20 minutes.
2   Turn the portions over, season again, sprinkle with Wor-
    cestershire sauce and return to the oven for a further 20
    minutes.

84

3   Meanwhile, trim and quarter the heads of fennel. Place in a saucepan with the onion and chicken stock, cover and cook gently until tender.
4   Pipe or fork the mashed potato in the centre of a warm serving dish. Surround with the chicken portions and drained fennel.
5   Add the chicken juices to the fennel stock. Moisten the cornflour with a little cold water and use to thicken the sauce. Cook for 2 minutes, stirring constantly. Season to taste and spoon over the chicken.

SERVES 4   Calories per portion 360 (360)

Gingered Kidney Casserole

450 g (1 lb) ox kidney
50 g (2 oz) Outline
275 ml (½ pint) slimmers' dry ginger ale
2.5 ml (½ teaspoon) ground ginger
Salt and black pepper

15 ml (1 tablespoon) vinegar
1 beef stock cube
15 ml (1 tablespoon) slimmers' black currant jam
15 ml (1 tablespoon) cornflour
30 ml (2 tablespoons) water

1   Trim and slice the kidney, remove hard core, and cut into small pieces.
2   Melt the Outline in a large saucepan. Use to fry the kidney gently until sealed on all sides. Add the ginger ale, ground ginger, seasoning, vinegar, crumbled stock cube and bring to the boil, stirring constantly.
3   Cover and simmer for 40 minutes, or until the kidney is tender. Stir in the jam until it is completely melted.
4   Moisten the cornflour with the water, add to the pan and bring back to the boil, stirring all the time. Cook for 2 minutes and adjust the seasoning if necessary.
5   Serve each portion with 100 g (4 oz) steamed cauliflower sprigs, sprinkled with chopped parsley.

SERVES 4   Calories per portion with vegetables 195 (210)

Curried Beef with Bananas

(See photograph pages 78–79)

450 g (1 lb) minced beef
2 medium-sized onions, peeled and chopped
1 cooking apple, peeled, cored and chopped
15–30 ml (1–2 tablespoons) curry powder
1.5 ml (¼ level teaspoon) ground ginger (optional)
1.5 ml (¼ level teaspoon) cinnamon (optional)
1.5 ml (¼ level teaspoon) ground cloves (optional)
396 g (14 oz) can tomatoes

275 ml (½ pint) water
Bay leaf
Salt and pepper, to taste
2 bananas, peeled and sliced
75 g (3 oz) boiled rice, per portion
1 green pepper, de-seeded and thinly sliced

SAMBALS

1 green pepper, de-seeded and thinly sliced, radishes sliced and mixed with natural yogurt, and peanuts

1   Fry minced beef gently in a pan for about 10 minutes, and drain off all the fat.
2   Add onion and apple to mince, and fry for 5 minutes.
3   Add curry powder and spices, and fry for 3 minutes.
4   Stir in tomatoes, water, bay leaf and seasoning.
5   Bring to boil, cover pan and simmer for 30 minutes stirring occasionally. Alternatively, the curry can be cooked in a covered casserole in a pre-heated oven 160°C 325°F, Gas 3.
6   Ten minutes before end of cooking time, add the banana and heat through.
7   Serve curry with boiled rice, accompanied by sambals (side dishes).

SERVES 4

Calories per portion with rice and vegetables (not including nuts) 345 (350)

Oven Chops Italienne

25 g (1 oz) Outline
1 large onion, finely sliced into
  rings
4 well-trimmed lamb chops
225 g (8 oz) mushrooms,
  chopped

185 g (6½ oz) can tomatoes
Salt and pepper
Good pinch oregano
15 g (½ oz) grated Parmesan
  cheese

1   Melt Outline over gentle heat and sauté onion rings until softened. Remove from pan.
2   Brown chops on both sides to seal.
3   Put chops and onion into an ovenproof casserole with chopped mushrooms. Pour over tomatoes and season well with salt, pepper and oregano. Cover.
4   Bake for 1 hour at 190°C 375°F, Gas 5. Remove lid, sprinkle with grated Parmesan cheese and cook for a further 15 minutes.
5   Serve with 1 small jacket potato per person plus a knob of Outline and braised celery.

SERVES 4   Calories per portion with vegetables 460 (460)

Green Pasta Bolognaise

(See photograph pages 78–79)

450 g (1 lb) minced beef
2 large onions, chopped
1 clove of garlic
2 sticks celery, chopped
Salt and pepper
425 ml (¾ pint) beef stock

50 g (2 oz) tomato paste
175 g (6 oz) green tagliatelle
269 g (9½ oz) can beansprouts,
  drained
10 ml (2 teaspoons) Parmesan
  cheese

1   Place the mince in a saucepan and fry for 5–8 minutes, draining off all the fat.
2   Add the onion, garlic, celery, seasoning, stock and tomato paste. Bring to the boil and simmer for 20–30 minutes.

3   Cook the tagliatelle in boiling salted water for 15 minutes. Add the beansprouts 1 minute before the tagliatelle is cooked. Drain.
4   Arrange the tagliatelle and beansprouts around the edge of a hot serving dish.
5   Pile the meat mixture in the centre and sprinkle over the Parmesan cheese.

SERVES 4   Calories per portion 420 (415)

Turkey in Mushroom Sauce

1 large onion, chopped
425 ml (¾ pint) dry cider
25 g (1 oz) Outline
175 g (6 oz) mushrooms, sliced
15 g (½ oz) flour
2.5 ml (½ teaspoon) prepared English mustard

Salt and pepper
450 g (1 lb) cooked turkey or chicken
30 ml (2 tablespoons) soured cream

1   Place the onion and cider in a saucepan and cook gently for 10 minutes.
2   Melt the Outline in another pan and use to sauté the mushrooms for 3 minutes. Stir in the flour and cook for a further minute.
3   Gradually add the cooked onion and cider liquid, bring to the boil, stirring constantly, until the sauce is smooth and thick. Stir in the mustard and season to taste.
4   Cut the turkey into large cubes and add to the sauce. Stir well and reheat to boiling point. Simmer for 2 minutes and stir in the cream.
5   Serve each person with a portion of the turkey in sauce and 100 g (4 oz) cooked Brussels sprouts tossed with 15 g (½ oz) Outline.

SERVES 4   Calories per portion with vegetable 360 (370)

Beef Olives
with Walnuts and Beansprouts

(See photograph pages 78–79)

1 small head celery
4 x 100 g (4 oz) thin slices beef
   skirt
100 g (4 oz) beansprouts
25 g (1 oz) chopped walnuts
2.5 ml (½ teaspoon) ground
   ginger

30 ml (2 tablespoons) soft
   breadcrumbs
50 g (2 oz) Outline, melted
Salt and pepper
30 ml (2 tablespoons) seasoned
   flour
275 ml (½ pint) beef stock

1 Trim and remove outer stalks of celery. Chop 4 stalks finely and quarter the heart. Beat out the slices of meat thinly.
2 Combine the beansprouts, walnuts, chopped celery, ginger and breadcrumbs with half the Outline.
3 Spread filling over the meat slices, season well, roll up and secure with white thread. Coat rolls in seasoned flour.
4 Sauté the beef rolls in the remaining Outline, turning frequently, until brown all over. Remove from the pan.
5 Add the rest of the seasoned flour to the fat remaining in the pan, stir well and add the stock. Bring to the boil, stirring constantly. Return the rolls to the pan, cover and simmer for about 30 minutes, or until the beef is tender.
6 Meanwhile, simmer the celery quarters in lightly salted water in a covered pan until tender.
7 Remove the threads from the beef olives.
8 Serve each person with 1 beef olive, 1 quarter of celery heart and 100 g (4 oz) boiled potatoes.

SERVES 4   Calories per portion with vegetables 460 (480)

Light Meals

Cheesey Stuffed Pancakes

FILLING

15 g (½ oz) Outline
100 g (4 oz) green beans, sliced
100 g (4 oz) mushrooms,
   chopped
1 medium-sized onion, chopped
275 ml (½ pint) basic
   All-in-One coating sauce
   (see basic recipe page 11)
50 g (2 oz) Edam cheese, grated

BATTER

100 g (4 oz) plain flour
Pinch of salt
1 standard egg
275 ml (½ pint) skimmed milk
Outline to fry pancakes

TOPPING

15 g (½ oz) Parmesan cheese,
   grated
2 tomatoes, sliced

1   Melt Outline and gently sauté beans, mushrooms and
    onion.
2   Prepare sauce and add grated Edam cheese.
3   Mix half sauce with vegetables.
4   To make the batter, place the flour and salt in a mixing
    bowl and make a hole in the centre. Add the egg and half
    the milk. Beat with a wooden spoon until smooth. Beat in
    remaining milk. Make 8 pancakes.
5   Divide filling between pancakes, and roll up the pancake
    to hold the filling.
6   Place the pancakes in an ovenproof dish, with the join
    downwards. Pour over the rest of the sauce. Sprinkle over
    the Parmesan cheese.
7   Put in pre-heated oven 200°C 400°F, Gas 6, for 15 minutes
    till heated through. Garnish with tomato and serve.

SERVES 4   Calories per portion 310 (335)

Fishy Potato Rounds

100 g (4 oz) smoked haddock,
  cooked and flaked
175 g (6 oz) potatoes, cooked
  and mashed

50 g (2 oz) plain flour
5 ml (1 teaspoon) mixed herbs
Salt and pepper
50 g (2 oz) Outline

1 Mix the flaked fish, potato, flour, herbs and seasoning together.
2 Turn the mixture onto a lightly floured surface and roll out to 2.5 cm (1 inch) thickness.
3 Cut into 8 rounds using a 6.5 cm (2½ inch) plain cutter.
4 Melt the Outline and fry the potato cakes on both sides until golden brown. Drain and serve.

SERVES 4   Calories per portion 145 (160)

Swiss Herrings

4 herrings
15 ml (1 tablespoon) French
  mustard
Salt and pepper
25 g (1 oz) Outline, melted

4 individual portions processed
  Swiss Gruyère cheese
Parsley and lemon slices, to
  garnish

1 Wash herrings, remove heads and clean. Split open and remove backbones.
2 Spread French mustard over flesh and season.
3 Fold body together again, brush with melted Outline and grill for 5 minutes.
4 Put a portion of Gruyère cheese on each herring and continue grilling gently until cheese has melted and fish is cooked.
5 Serve garnished with parsley and lemon slices.

SERVES 4   Calories per portion 315 (320)

Desserts

Two-fruits Pudding

(See photograph page 80)

1 quantity Victoria Sandwich
Cake mixture (see basic recipe
page 13) with grated rind and
juice of 1 lemon added to
ingredients before mixing.
2 oranges, sliced

ORANGE SAUCE

10 ml (2 teaspoon) arrowroot
150 ml (¼ pint) slimmers'
orange drink
150 ml (¼ pint) water
2.5 ml (½ teaspoon) lemon juice

1 Prepare cake mixture.
2 Place the orange slices around the bottom and sides of a
1 litre (2 pint) greased pudding basin.
3 Carefully place the cake mixture over the fruit.
4 Cover with foil or greased greaseproof paper and steam
over fast boiling water for 1¼–2 hours.
5 Meanwhile make the orange sauce. Place all the ingredients in a small saucepan and bring to the boil over low
heat, stirring constantly, until sauce thickens and clears.
6 Turn out and serve hot with a little sauce poured over and
the rest served separately.

SERVES 8 Calories for whole pudding (with sauce) 2350
(2295)
Calories for ⅛ pudding (with sauce) 295 (290)

Princess Pudding

(See photograph page 80)

40 g (1½ oz) soft breadcrumbs
15 g (½ oz) Outline
Artificial liquid sweetener to
taste
425 ml (¾ pint) skimmed milk

Grated rind of ½ lemon
2 standard eggs, separated
Few drops vanilla essence
30 ml (2 tablespoons) slimmers'
jam

92

1   Place crumbs, Outline and liquid sweetener in a bowl.
2   Warm milk gently and pour over crumbs.
3   Cool slightly and beat in lemon rind, egg yolks and vanilla essence.
4   Pour mixture into a 900 ml (1 ½ pint) ovenproof dish and bake in centre of pre-heated oven 180°C 350°F, Gas 4, for 20 minutes until set.
5   Spread top with jam.
6   Whisk egg whites stiffly. Pile on top of pudding and grill for a few minutes until meringue is set and browned.

SERVES 4   Calories per portion 130 (125)

Eve's Temptation Apples

(See photograph page 80)

2 large cooking apples
30 ml (2 tablespoons) water
5 ml (1 teaspoon) lemon juice
Artificial liquid sweetener to
   taste

3 thin slices white bread
50 g (2 oz) Outline
50 g (2 oz) demerara sugar
Grated rind of 1 lemon

1   Peel, core and slice the apples.
2   Cook the apple in the water and lemon juice until soft. Add sweetener to taste.
3   Meanwhile, spread the bread with most of the Outline, reserving a little for the topping. Remove the crusts and set aside. Cut the bread into fingers.
4   Line an ovenproof dish with the fingers, spread side out-wards. Pour the cooked apple into the centre, and lay the crusts on top.
5   Mix together the sugar and lemon rind, sprinkle over the dish and dot with the rest of the Outline. Bake at 200°C 400°F, Gas 6, for 20 minutes.

SERVES 4   Calories per portion 165 (170)

93

Moist Banana Tea Bread

(See photograph page 80)

50 g (2 oz) Outline
3 medium bananas, mashed
100 g (4 oz) castor sugar
1 large egg

Grated rind of 1 orange
50 g (2 oz) walnuts, chopped
275 g (10 oz) self-raising flour
2.5 ml (½ level teaspoon) salt

1 Place all the ingredients in a mixing bowl and beat together with a wooden spoon until well mixed (2–3 minutes).
2 Line the bottom of a 900 g (2 lb) loaf tin with greaseproof paper. Grease the tin, and place the mixture in it. Smooth the top.
3 Bake on the middle shelf of a pre-heated oven 180°C 350°F, Gas 4, for 1¼–1½ hours. Cool on a wire tray.
4 Serve sliced, spread thinly with Outline.

MAKES 16 SLICES Calories per slice without Outline 150 (160) with Outline 180 (190)

Meringue Nests

4 pear halves canned in natural juice
1.25 ml (¼ teaspoon) ground nutmeg
100 g (4 oz) frozen raspberries, defrosted

5 ml (1 teaspoon) arrowroot
Few drops artificial liquid sweetener
4 meringue nests

1 Drain the pear halves well and place on absorbent paper.
2 Place the pear juice in a pan with the nutmeg and boil rapidly until reduced by half.
3 Sieve the raspberries and stir the purée into the reduced pear liquid. Moisten the arrowroot with a little cold water, add to the pan and bring to the boil. Cook, stirring, until the sauce thickens and clears. Add liquid sweetener to taste. Cool.
4 Arrange the pear halves in the meringue nests and glaze with the spicy raspberry sauce.

SERVES 4 Calories per filled nest 100 (100)

Winter Ideas

1 When you plan your Christmas catering, make at least one cake you can enjoy without damaging your diet. Use the All-in-One Victoria Sandwich Cake recipe on page 13. Reserve half the filling and use it to ice the top of the cake. Add a plastic robin or Father Christmas in his sleigh complete with reindeer to keep the energy content down!

2 Out-of-door activities in cold weather are more beneficial than at any other time of the year because we use more energy keeping warm.

3 If this is the season when you find it specially difficult to contemplate a weight reducing diet, first try eating normally, but reduce every portion by one-third. This ought to inspire you to take the diet plunge because most of us crowd our plates with food supposedly to keep out the cold.

4 To keep warm, plan to do the housework twice as fast as usual. This gets it out of the way and leaves time for more exciting things.

5 If you plan a Continental holiday, brush up on the local language by playing the appropriate language tape or record while you are busy with some physical chore such as polishing. You do not always need to sit still while listening.

Winter Drinks

JAMAICAN COFFEE

To a cup of hot black coffee, add a few drops of rum essence and liquid sweetener to taste.

PEPPERMINT COLA

Place a few drops of peppermint essence in the bottom of a tall glass and fill with slimmers' cola. Stir well and serve with a lemon slice hooked over the side of the glass.

Take entertaining in your stride

Resist the temptation to abandon your diet plan completely if you are entertaining at home, or invited out by friends. There is always an alternative to the embarrassment of refusing a tempting dish or obviously eating something different from everyone else at the table.

SURVIVING THE SOCIAL STRAIN

Every dieter has encountered at one time or another the problem of being offered delicious food which is terribly difficult to refuse. If your hostess has obviously taken great trouble to cook for you and is proud of the result, how can you refuse without offending her? In this situation you must make up your mind to compromise by taking the smallest portion possible, unobtrusively leaving a little on your plate, or compensate by cutting down your food intake for a day or two afterwards. Small tricks help to minimize the problem. No one will notice if you refuse a roll or French bread and butter, or scoop a thick layer of creamy sauce or mayonnaise off the starter before eating it. Be determined enough to refuse offers of second helpings of anything but an innocuous salad. Have soda water and a slice of lemon instead of an apéritif. At table, once your wineglass is filled, drink only a sip and no one will insist on filling it up. If your hostess offers cheese as an extra course, it never gives offence to refuse it, whereas she might be really hurt if she has taken a great deal of trouble to concoct a fancy dessert which you turn down without any apparent reason.

At a restaurant, you will probably be able to take your choice of the menu, and make sure the meal is within your diet allowance. An exotic starter can be totally avoided since most restaurants serve consommé, or some other kind of clear soup, juices, and melon. Tomato juice spiked with Worcestershire sauce is an excellent choice. If you can influence your host's choice, mention that you like a Moselle, or another dry white wine. Of the reds, a claret is preferable. Ask for a glass of water as well and then you won't be so tempted to drink the wine quickly. Grilled white fish would be a good main course to choose, rather than fish à la Meunière. Fish goes well with spinach, petits pois or green beans. And for dessert, a fresh pineapple slice with Kirsch – you may be sure you will not get too much liqueur. Black coffee without milk or cream should be no problem, even if you have to unobtrusively pop in your artificial sweetener. When entertainment takes the form of a simple get-together in the pub, you can at least ask for a slimmers' drink, with ice and a slice of lemon. Who knows there is neither vodka nor gin in it? When a jovial host presses you to accept something more cheerful, remember a measure of your favourite spirit with a slimmers' mixer or a glass of dry white wine is best for dieters.

ENTERTAINING AT HOME – PLEASING GUESTS WITHOUT HARMING YOUR DIET

The great advantage of eating at home is that you are in complete control of the food. This also applies to alcoholic drinks, always a deceptive source of surplus energy. When a welcoming drink is offered to friends you can tactfully be 'too busy' greeting them to join in. At table, where the choice of starter is yours, it need never be loaded with oil or cream. Melon can be prettily presented in so many ways, it makes an ideal starter at any time of the year. Your grapefruit half can be sprinkled with liquid sweetener instead of sugar. Your shellfish starter can be topped with a slimmers' dressing or seasoned yogurt instead of mayonnaise. Very thin brown bread spread with Outline will please everyone at the table, or you can press it into small individual pots, and scrape the surface flat, as they do in French restaurants. When it comes to the main course, it is not essential to pour over a very rich sauce before serving it. If the basic dish is a slimmer's delight, the accompaniments can be rich: potato slices baked in cream, or a vegetable smothered in cheese sauce. As it is a compliment to the guests to offer a selection of vegetables, and frequently a salad as well, you can always make your personal choice a sensible one. Tiny boiled carrots glistening with melted Outline and sprinkled with parsley, for instance, are far from disastrous. It flatters your guests if you offer a choice of desserts. One of these could always be a fresh fruit salad moistened with unsweeted orange juice. It is so delicious that guests may even choose this in preference to your Creamy Mousse or Baked Alaska, and for them provide a bowl of whipped cream to go with it.

Just to show how easy it is, here are two party menus to help you entertain at home in style, without breaking the diet rules yourself.

Outdoor buffet for eight

Turkey Pots
Pasta Salad with Fish
Outline Garlic Bread
Raspberry Cheesecake

Turkey Pots

Few sprigs fresh tarragon
450 g (1 lb) cooked white turkey
* meat*
Salt and black pepper

30 ml (2 tablespoons) lemon juice
50 g (2 oz) Outline
Shredded lettuce
1 large lemon

1   Strip the leaves from the tarragon and chop them.
2   Mince the turkey, season and add the lemon juice and chopped tarragon.
3   Pound the meat mixture until smooth and creamy, and work in the Outline.
4   Divide the mixture between 8 ramekin dishes or foil containers and press down well. Chill.
5   Make a bed of shredded lettuce on a flat platter and turn the turkey pots out on this. Cut the lemon into 8 wedges and use to garnish the dish.

SERVES 8   Calories per portion 125 (130)

Pasta Salad with Fish

(See photograph page 37)

450 g (1 lb) small pasta shapes
225 g (8 oz) mushrooms
50 g (2 oz) Outline
2 x 200 g (7 oz) cans tuna

60 ml (4 tablespoons) slimmers'
    salad dressing
2 lettuces
16 cooked fresh or canned
    asparagus spears

1   Cook the pasta in boiling salted water. Drain, rinse in cold
    water and drain again.
2   Reserve 8 whole mushroom caps for the garnish and slice
    the remainder. Sauté them all in the Outline until pale
    golden. Cool.
3   Drain the tuna and combine the liquid with the salad
    dressing. Flake the fish, mix with the pasta, sliced mush-
    rooms and dressing.
4   Reserve 8 large lettuce leaves for cups and shred the
    remainder. Arrange the shredded lettuce on a platter or in
    individual bowls.
5   Fill the lettuce cups with the salad mixture and arrange in
    bowls or on the platter. Decorate the top with cooked
    asparagus spears.
6   Garnish each lettuce cup of salad with a mushroom cap.

SERVES 8   Calories per portion 385 (390)

Outline Garlic Bread

2 small Vienna loaves, or short
    French sticks
100 g (4 oz) Outline

3 cloves of garlic, crushed, and a
    little salt
OR 15 ml (1 tablespoon) garlic
    salt

1   Slice through the loaves almost to the base at 2.5 cm
    (1 inch) intervals.
2   Beat together Outline, garlic and salt (or garlic salt).
3   Spread this mixture on both sides of each cut in the loaves.
    Press together to re-shape the loaves and wrap in foil.
4   Heat in oven at 200°C 400°F, Gas 6, for 20 minutes.

SERVES 8   Calories per slice 100 (100)

Raspberry Cheesecake

(See photograph page 40)

BASE
15 g (½ oz) Outline
4 digestive biscuits, crushed

FILLING
15 g (½ oz) gelatine
45 ml (3 tablespoons) water

227 g (8 oz) cottage cheese,
    sieved
2 x 150 g (5.3 oz) cartons
    low-fat raspberry yogurt

DECORATION
100g (4 oz) fresh raspberries

1 Grease the inside of a 15 cm (6 inch) loose-bottomed cake tin with the Outline.
2 Coat the inside of the tin with the biscuit crumbs.
3 Dissolve the gelatine in the water in a basin over hot water.
4 Mix dissolved gelatine, cottage cheese and yogurt, and pour into base. Leave to set.
5 When set, remove from tin and decorate with raspberries.

SERVES 8   Calories per portion 75 (75)

Dinner party for four

Orange Cress Crunch
Noisettes of Lamb with Pineapple
Marbled Cranberry Dessert

WINE TO GO WITH THE MENU

Dry white wine would be a perfect accompaniment to lamb and is lower in calories than either sweet white or red wines. A slimmers' ginger ale is not very different in colour and if you are being very strict about your diet, you could serve yourself with this instead.

COFFEE TO END THE MEAL

Make a little ceremony of serving extra special coffee such as Viennese fig coffee, taken black of course by you. Forego milk or cream, even if you usually take white coffee. Extra artificial sweetening makes black coffee much more acceptable.

Orange Cress Crunch

1 punnet mustard and cress
100 g (4 oz) beansprouts
2 small frankfurter sausages
1 large orange
1 small slice slimmers' bread
25 g (1 oz) Outline

DRESSING

15 ml (1 tablespoon) vinegar
Salt and pepper
2.5 ml (½ teaspoon) French
  mustard

1   Snip the cress, wash carefully and drain well. Snip up the beansprouts. Slice the frankfurters diagonally in 2.5 cm (1 inch) lengths. Peel and segment the orange.
2   Place all these ingredients together in a salad bowl.
3   Trim and cut the bread into small dice. Melt the Outline and use to fry the bread cubes gently until golden brown.
4   Make the dressing. Season the vinegar with the mustard, and salt and pepper to taste.
5   Toss the bread dice with the orange salad mixture while still warm, pour over the dressing and toss again lightly.
6   Serve each person with a portion of the crunchy salad in a small glass dish.

SERVES 4   Calories per portion 145 (150)

Noisettes of Lamb with Pineapple

Small bunch parsley
25 g (1 oz) Outline
5 ml (1 teaspoon) clear honey
5 ml (1 teaspoon) dry mustard
1 clove garlic, crushed

227 g (8 oz) can pineapple slices
  in natural juice
Salt and pepper
8 noisettes of lamb, tied with
  white string

1   Chop 30 ml (2 tablespoons) parsley, and reserve the remaining sprigs for the garnish.
2   Melt the Outline and mix with the honey, mustard, chopped parsley and garlic. Add the juice from the can of pineapple and season to taste.

3   Brush the noisettes with some of the Outline mixture and grill for about 5–6 minutes on each side, basting frequently with the mixture, until golden brown and cooked through.
4   Meanwhile, cut the pineapple rings in half and heat gently in the remaining Outline mixture.
5   Arrange the noisettes on a warm platter, each propped up on half a slice of pineapple, spooning any remaining sauce over the top. Garnish with the parsley sprigs.
6   Serve each person with 2 noisettes and pineapple and 100 g (4 oz) broccoli spears garnished with finely sliced radish. For non-slimmers add an extra noisette and extra pineapple.

SERVES 4   Calories per portion with vegetable 388 (385)

Marbled Cranberry Dessert

1 raspberry flavoured packet jelly
2 dessert apples, peeled
2 medium bananas, mashed

175 g (6 oz) jar or can cranberry sauce
275 ml (½ pint) fruit-flavoured yogurt

1   Make up the jelly to half strength and cool until syrupy.
2   Grate the apples, and mash the bananas. Beat the cranberry sauce until smooth, and fold in the apple and banana.
3   Whisk the jelly until foamy and fold in the cranberry mixture.
4   Swirl the yogurt lightly through the jelly to give a marbled effect. Turn into a large glass dish or 4 wine glasses and chill until firm.

SERVES 4   Calories per portion 315 (315)

Three Diet Plans

Plan A is designed to produce a slightly faster loss in weight than Plan B. Plan C is for those who lead a very strenuous life.

PLAN A – 1250 CALORIE DIET

	CALORIES
Breakfast	200
Starter or dessert	200
Main meal (choose from those with lower calorie counts)	400
Light meal	300
275 ml (½ pint) skimmed milk (half for cooking/half for drinks)	100
One fruit plus 2–3 nibbles	50
	1250

PLAN B – 1550 CALORIE DIET

	CALORIES
Breakfast	200
Starter or dessert	200
Main meal	500
Light meal	300
275 ml (½ pint) skimmed milk (half for cooking/half for drinks)	100
Two fruits plus 2–3 nibbles	100
One 'Funsize' candy bar *or* 1 small All-in-One Scone (see page 12) lightly spread with Outline *or* 1 small slice All-in-One Victoria Sandwich (see page 13) with Creamy Filling (page 14)	150
	1550

	CALORIES
Breakfast	200
Starter	200
Main meal	500
Dessert	200
Light meal	300
275 ml (½ pint) skimmed milk (half for cooking/half for drinks)	100
275 ml (½ pint) beer	
or 1 dry sherry	
or 1 glass dry wine	100
Two fruits plus 2–3 nibbles	100
One 'Funsize' candy bar	
or 1 small All-in-One Scone (see page 12) lightly spread with Outline	
or 1 small slice All-in-One Victoria Sandwich (see page 13) with Creamy Filling (page 14)	150
	1850

Your Guide to Joules and Calories

The chart on page 106 is a guide to the energy content of the food and drinks you include in your diet. The energy contents are listed in both kilojoules and kilocalories to help you become familiar with the new unit, the kilojoule.

Along with measures such as the foot, the pound and the pint, the calorie is due to be replaced by the joule. The joule, like the calorie, is simply a measurement of energy, and is the method used with the Système International d'Unités (SI). The energy content in the future will be measured in kilojoules. We shall also be referring to joule-controlled diets.

One kilocalorie is equivalent to 4.2 kilojoules. For converting from kilocalories to kilojoules all you need to do is multiply by 4.2. For example, a caorie-controlled diet of 1000 kilocalories will become a joule-controlled diet of 4200 kilojoules. A 10 kilocalorie tomato will become a 42 kilojoule tomato.

The Outline Slimming Bureau

The Outline Slimming Bureau was set up in 1971 to help people with their weight problems.

We know that handing a diet sheet to someone who wants to slim is not enough. If losing weight meant merely adhering to a recommended 'dose of joules (calories) three times a day' there would be no need for the advisory service we run.

No two slimmers think they share the same needs but what they usually have in mind is a longing for encouragement – to start dieting and even more so to keep going over what may turn out to be many long months. And this is where the Bureau comes in. You can telephone us or we can help you by post. If you would like any information about slimming then drop us a line, on a post-card if you can. We always do our best to find out what will help *you*, the individual, to lose weight and stay at a healthy weight. Through talking to slimmers over the years and initiating diet research trials we have learnt a lot about the pitfalls and misunderstandings that slimmers invariably encounter. At the Bureau we do our best to guide you through a successful and, we hope, enjoyable weight reducing plan.

We have a range of free publications available on request from the Bureau at the address below. These booklets cover the facts about losing and controlling weight, how to set about planning and following a weight reducing diet. We also have a series of leaflets produced specially for expectant mothers, pre-teenage children and men. We can send you more calorie counted recipes, exercise ideas, a height/weight guide cum weight loss record chart to prompt you to gloat over the disappearing pounds each week.

The Bureau has compiled a 'Slimmer's Kit' for adults who would like to join up with overweight colleagues, friends or members of the family and benefit from the support of a group. Our fourteen minute colour film 'Outline of Slimming' could be useful here but you will need to locate a 16 mm sound projector and an experienced operator to run it for you.

So remember that whether your weight problem is big or small, of years standing or recent we think we can help you help yourself to slim successfully *this* time. Contact us at Outline Slimming Bureau, Sussex House, Burgess Hill, West Sussex, RH15 9AW.

Joule/Calorie Chart

The values given are an approximate guide to the energy content of food

	Quantity	Kilo-joules	Kilo-calories
Bread			
Small brown or white slice	1	250	60
Small slice fried	1	585	140
Crispbreads (depending on variety)	1	105	25
Breakfast cereals			
All Bran	1 oz	370	90
	100 g	1330	318
Cornflakes, Rice Crispies	1 oz	418	100
	100 g	1475	353
Müesli, average	1 oz	460	110
	100 g	1625	388
Cereals and other flour based products			
Cornflour, custard powder	1 oz	418	100
	100 g	1475	353
Flour, white	1 oz	414	99
	100 g	1455	348
Pasta, raw macaroni	1 oz	431	103
	100 g	1525	365
raw spaghetti	1 oz	431	103
	100 g	1525	365
Pastry, cooked flaky	1 oz	699	167
	100 g	2462	589
cooked shortcrust	1 oz	656	157
	100 g	2318	554
Rice, raw	1 oz	427	102
	100 g	1505	360
boiled or steamed	1 oz	146	35
	100 g	519	124
Cheese			
Cheddar	1 oz	490	117
	100 g	1725	413
Cheshire	1 oz	460	110
	100 g	1625	388
Cottage	1 oz	138	32
	100 g	472	113
Cream	1 oz	544	130
	100 g	1920	459
Curd	1 oz	167	40
	100 g	590	142
Edam	1 oz	348	88
	100 g	1298	313

	Quantity	Kilo-joules	Kilo-calories
Drinks – Other beverages			
Chocolate and malted drinks	½ pint	840	200
	275 ml	808	194
Coffee black without sugar	1 cup	4	1
white, half milk	1 cup	334	80
half milk, with sugar	1 cup	434	104
Tea without milk or sugar	1 cup	4	1
with milk	1 cup	84	20
with milk and sugar	1 cup	184˙	44
Eggs, standard			
Boiled eggs	1	334	80
Fried eggs	1	570	136
Omelette	2	954	228
Poached	1	334	80
Scrambled	1	503	120
White of egg	1	63	15
Yolk of egg	1	272	65
Fats and oils			
Butter	1 oz	878	210
	100 g	3096	741
Cooking fat	1 oz	1062	254
	100 g	3680	898
Cooking oil	1 oz	1066	255
	100 g	3762	900
Margarine	1 oz	878	210
	100 g	3096	741
Outline low-fat spread	1 oz	440	105
	100 g	1550	371
Fish and shellfish			
Anchovies	1 fillet	29	7
Cockles, shelled	1 oz	59	14
	100 g	203	49
Fishfingers	1 finger	210	50
Herring, raw	1 oz	276	66
	100 g	973	232
Oily fish, eg. mackerel, sardines,	1 oz	210	50
kipper, raw	100 g	738	176
Mussels, shelled	1 oz	103	25
	100 g	369	88
Shellfish, eg. prawns, crab, shrimp	1 oz	125	30
	100 g	443	106
Salmon, canned	1 oz	184	44
	100 g	650	155
Trout, baked on bone	1 oz	125	30
	100 g	443	106
White fish, eg. cod, haddock,	1 oz	88	21
plaice, raw	100 g	310	74

	Quantity	Kilo-joules	Kilo-calories
Fruit and nuts			
Apple, small eating	1	167	40
Apricot, canned in syrup	1 oz	125	30
	100 g	443	106
Avocado, medium	½	523	125
Banana, weighed with skin	150 g/5 oz	209	65
Blackberries, fresh	1 oz	34	8
	100 g	118	28
Cherries, fresh with stones	1 oz	59	14
	100 g	206	49
Coconut, desiccated	1 oz	723	173
	100 g	2553	611
Dates, dried with stones	1 oz	255	61
	100 g	900	215
Gooseberries, stewed with	1 oz	17	4
artificial sweetener	100 g	59	14
Grapefruit, fresh	½	104	25
Grapes	1 oz	59	14
	100 g	206	49
Mandarin oranges, canned in syrup	1 oz	75	18
	100 g	268	64
Melon, one slice	150 g/5 oz	84	20
Nuts, eg. almonds, walnuts, peanuts	1 oz	685	164
	100 g	2422	580
Orange, fresh	150 g/5 oz	209	50
Peach, fresh	150 g/5 oz	230	55
Peanuts, shelled and roasted	1 oz	695	166
	100 g	2450	586
Pear, fresh	150 g/5 oz	251	60
Pineapple, canned in syrup	1 oz	92	22
	100 g	336	80
Plums, stewed with artificial	1 oz	29	7
sweetener	100 g	104	25
Prunes, dried with stone	1 oz	159	38
	100 g	561	134
Raisins, sultanas	1 oz	293	70
	100 g	1032	247
Raspberries, fresh	1 oz	29	7
	100 g	103	25
Rhubarb, stewed with artificial	1 oz	8	2
sweetener	100 g	30	7
Strawberries, fresh	1 oz	33	8
	100 g	117	28
Meat			
Bacon, streaky, raw	1 oz	502	120
	100 g	1774	424
Bacon, back, raw	1 oz	418	100
	100 g	1475	353
Beefburger	1	669	160

	Quantity	Kilo-joules	Kilo-calories
Beef, grilling steak, raw	1 oz	209	50
	100 g	735	176
Beef, stewing steak or lean mince	1 oz	251	60
	100 g	886	212
Chicken, roast, no bones	1 oz	209	50
	100 g	735	176
Corned beef	1 oz	255	61
	100 g	898	215
Duck, roast, no bones	1 oz	251	60
	100 g	886	212
Gammon steak, grilled	1 oz	251	60
	100 g	886	212
Kidney, raw	1 oz	125	30
	100 g	443	106
Lamb, roast leg, meat only	1 oz	334	80
	100 g	1178	282
Lamb chop, weighed raw, grilled	6 oz	1003	240
	175 g	995	248
Liver, pig's, raw	1 oz	188	45
	100 g	665	159
Pork chop, weighed raw, grilled	6 oz	1252	300
	175 g	1290	309
Pork, roast, meat only	1 oz	376	90
	100 g	1329	318
Pork, sausage, raw	1 oz	418	100
	100 g	1475	353
Rabbit, raw, with bone	1 oz	130	37
	100 g	546	131
Sweetbreads, stewed	1 oz	209	50
	100 g	740	177
Tongue, pressed	1 oz	356	85
	100 g	1253	300
Veal, roast, lean	1 oz	272	65
	100 g	958	229

Milk and milk products

	Quantity	Kilo-joules	Kilo-calories
Cream, double	1 fl oz	532	127
	100 g	1885	448
Cream, single	1 fl oz	226	54
	100 g	800	191
Cream, soured	1 fl oz	226	54
	100 g	800	191
Milk, condensed sweetened	1 fl oz	380	91
	100 g	1341	321
Milk, dried skimmed	1 oz	418	100
	100 g	1475	353
Milk, evaporated	1 fl oz	193	46
	100 g	678	162
Milk, fresh whole	½ pint	795	190
	275 ml	770	184

	Quantity	Kilo-joules	Kilo-calories
Yogurt, fruited	141 g – 5 oz carton approx	586	140
Yogurt, natural	141 g – 5 oz carton approx	314	75

Preserves

	Quantity	Kilo-joules	Kilo-calories
Honey	1 oz	392	82
	100 g	1209	389
Jam, marmalade	1 oz	309	74
	100 g	1090	261
Syrup	1 oz	351	84
	100 g	1238	296
White sugar	1 oz	468	112
	100 g	1654	396

Vegetables

	Quantity	Kilo-joules	Kilo-calories
Artichoke hearts, canned	1 oz	42	10
	100 g	148	35
Asparagus, boiled	1 oz	21	5
	100 g	75	18
Aubergine, raw	1 oz	17	4
	100 g	59	14
Baked beans in tomato sauce	1 oz	71	17
	100 g	251	60
Beans, broad, cooked	1 oz	50	12
	100 g	176	42
Beans, green, cooked	1 oz	8	2
	100 g	29	7
Beans, haricot, dried	1 oz	306	73
	100 g	1078	258
Beansprouts, raw	1 oz	34	8
	100 g	118	28
Beetroot, boiled	1 oz	50	12
	100 g	176	46
Broccoli, boiled	1 oz	17	4
	100 g	59	14
Brussels sprouts, boiled	1 oz	21	5
	100 g	75	18
Cabbage, boiled	1 oz	21	5
	100 g	75	18
Carrots, boiled	1 oz	25	6
	100 g	89	21
Cauliflower, boiled	1 oz	13	3
	100 g	46	11
Celery, raw	1 oz	13	3
	100 g	46	11
Celery, boiled	1 oz	4	1
	100 g	15	4
Chicory, raw	One head	42	10

	Quantity	Kilo-joules	Kilo-calories
Courgettes, raw	1 oz	13	3
	100 g	46	11
Cucumber, raw	1 oz	8	2
	100 g	29	7
Fennel, raw root	1 oz	29	7
	100 g	102	26
Gherkins, pickled	1 oz	13	3
	100 g	46	11
Leeks, boiled	1 oz	29	7
	100 g	102	26
Lentils, dried	1 oz	352	84
	100 g	1240	296
Marrow, raw, flesh only	1 oz	13	3
	100 g	46	11
Mushrooms, raw	1 oz	8	2
	100 g	29	7
Mustard and cress	1 oz	13	3
	100 g	46	11
Olives, black with stones	1	34	8
Onion, raw	1 oz	29	7
	100 g	102	26
Onion, pickled	1 large	29	7
Parsnips, raw	1 oz	59	14
	100 g	208 g	49
Peas, fresh or frozen, raw	1 oz	75	18
	100 g	268	64
Peas, canned	1 oz	92	22
	100 g	326	78
Pepper, green, raw	1 oz	17	4
	100 g	59	14
Potato crisps	1 oz	665	159
	100 g	2348	561
Potatoes, boiled	1 oz	96	23
	100 g	339	81
Potatoes, chipped	1 oz	284	68
	100 g	1003	240
Potatoes, roast	1 oz	134	32
	100 g	473	113
Spinach, raw	1 oz	25	6
	100 g	89	21
Spring greens	1 oz	13	11
	100 g	46	11
Swede, raw	1 oz	21	5
	100 g	75	18
Sweetcorn, canned	1 oz	92	22
	100 g	326	78
Tomatoes, raw	1 oz	13	3
	100 g	46	11
Turnips, raw	1 oz	21	5
	100 g	75	18

Index of Recipes

All-in-One Sauces, 11
All-in-One Scones, 12
All-in-One Victoria Sandwich, 13
Apple Curry Sauce on Baked Ham, 67
Avocado and Grapefruit Cups, 22
Baked Celery in Sherry Sauce, 24
Banana Rings, 33
Barbecued Pork Pockets, 45
Beet Olives with Walnuts and
    Beansprouts, 89
Beef Sausages with Cranberry Glaze, 72
Beefy Beetroot Soup, 82
Blackberry Baked Apples, 73
Black Cherry Gateau, 54
Breton Lamb, 28
Brussels Sprout Soup, 83
Cheesey Melon Wedges, 62
Cheesey Pasta with Kidneys, 29
Cheesey Stuffed Pancakes, 90
Chicken and Cucumber, 68
Chicken Liver Pâté, 24
Chicken Portions with Fennel, 84
Chilled Green Pea Soup, 42
Chocolate Fairy Cakes, 54
Choux Pastry, 14
Chunky Veal Soup, 50
Coffee Chiffon, 32
Cold Courgette Salad, 42
Consommé with Tropical Garnish, 22
Creamy Filling, 14
Creamy Topping, 32
Crispy Stuffed Tomatoes, 64
Crispy-Topped Marrow, 72
Curried Beef with Banana, 86
Easy Paella, 49
Eve's Temptation Apples, 93
Fish Knots, 69
Fish Mousse, 23
Fishy Potato Rounds, 91
Florentine Fish with Parsley Pats, 30
Fruit Jellies with Creamy Topping, 33
Fruity Rabbit Casserole, 48
Gammon with Fresh Apricot Sauce, 25
Gingered Kidney Casserole, 85
Golden Vegetable Soup, 82
Gooseberry Mint Snow, 53

Grape Salad with Toasted Coconut, 74
Greek Cheese Salad, 62
Green Pasta Bolognaise, 87
Harlequin Chicken Salad, 69
Hawaiian Gammon Rashers, 66
Herbed Cucumber Omelette, 51
Hot Baked Chicken with Artichoke Salad,
    27
Kitchen Garden Curry, 46
Lamb in Caper Sauce, 48
Lemon Veal Kebabs, 47
Mandarin Eclairs, 34
Marbled Cranberry Dessert, 102
Marinated Lamb Skewers, 65
Meringue Nests, 94
Moist Banana Tea Bread, 94
Noisettes of Lamb with Pineapple,
    101
Ocean Toasties, 30
Orange Cress Crunch, 101
Orange Parsley Chicken, 66
Outline Garlic Bread, 99
Oven Chops Italienne, 87
Pasta Salad with Fish, 99
Peach and Strawberry Fluff, 52
Pipérade with Eggs, 70
Piquant Fish, 68
Pizza Deliziosa, 71
Plum and Rhubarb with Hazelnut Crust,
    74
Princess Pudding, 92
Raspberry Cheesecake, 100
Red and Black Currant Ice, 52
Rhubarb and Ginger Crunch, 31
Seafood Cocktail, 43
Sicilian Veal Roast, 44
Slim Beef Casserole, 26
Stuffed Mackerel, 28
Super Celery Salad, 63
Swiss Herrings, 91
Tomato and Celery Soup, 84
Tomato and Tuna Jelly, 50
Turkey Escalopes with Mint, 45
Turkey in Mushroom Sauce, 88
Turkey Pots, 98
Two-fruits Pudding, 92